Charles S. Nickerson

Noble Living

Charles S. Nickerson

Noble Living

ISBN/EAN: 9783337780074

Printed in Europe, USA, Canada, Australia, Japan

Cover: Foto ©Thomas Meinert / pixelio.de

More available books at **www.hansebooks.com**

A SERIES OF STUDIES AS TO THE DEVELOPMENT
OF THE DEEPER LIFE IN MEN

EDITED BY

CHARLES SUMNER NICKERSON

———

BOSTON
UNIVERSALIST PUBLISHING HOUSE
1896

"*I am come that they might have life, and that they might have it more abundantly.*" — JESUS CHRIST.

"*Forgetting those things which are behind, and reaching forth unto those things which are before, I press toward the mark for the prize of the high calling of God in Christ Jesus.*" — ST. PAUL.

"*He who understands life deeply and fully, understands life truly — he has forever renewed his life; and if there comes into our hearts, in the life which we are living, a perpetual sense that life needs renewal, a richening and refreshing, then it is in order that we may go down into the depths and see what lies at the root of things — things that we are perpetually doing and thinking. It is that we may open to ourselves some newer, higher life.*" — PHILLIPS BROOKS.

PREFACE.

MEN are living in the midst of transient things. By necessity the mind is much occupied with the affairs of the present. While it is undoubtedly true that scores of our fellows are unnecessarily "*anxious* for the morrow," it cannot be denied that there is a demand laid upon every one to make some provision for the future. There must be nourishment, clothing, and shelter.

But because a man recognizes these requirements, he need not be blind to all things else. Even if he exist in a world of change, it is possible that he may be a partaker of the unchangeable. If he be compelled to deal with material things from day to day, it is possible that he may consider and utilize something which is not material. If his nature links him to lower ranges of activity, it also links him to the higher ranges. Though one lives in the world, he may be above the world.

The purpose of these Essays is to aid the soul in its struggle for attainment. The mountain of character is difficult to climb. From its summit alone can a clear view of life — its toils, duties, and fulfilment — be obtained. Multitudes tire even of the first attempt to rise. Many who spend years grasping at some slight out-jutting points, thereby making slow ascent, become weary of the undertaking and fall backward. Others, through the new motive furnished by the larger horizon, persist in their endeavor, and, though it be by winding ways and over rugged paths, enter into the joy of the wider apprehension.

To point to the heights, to indicate the opportunity and demand for ascent, to explain how struggle affords strength for continued effort; to present the helps and helpers beside the pathway, to suggest the practices whereby motive is developed, and to exhibit the motive itself; to prove existence a unit, to show what its constant upward movement signifies, and to guide to that condition wherein, amidst the rarer atmosphere of the Father's recognized presence, the soul is transfigured, — this is the design of the writers and of the editor.

May it please the Most Gracious Spirit to let his blessing attend this work, and may it aid to the fulfilment of the petition, "Thy will be done on earth as it is in heaven."

CONTENTS.

vii

WALKING WITH GOD.

CHARLES HENRY EATON.

WALKING WITH GOD.

WHEN, forty years ago, Pierre Leroux offered his article, "Dieu," to the *Revue des Deux Mondes*, it was returned with the observation, "The question of God lacks actuality." The old order was based upon Christian theism. Civilization has taken the place of Christianity; faith and hope in man, of faith and hope in God. As some one has said, "Vortex reigns in place of Zeus." The flippant and even scurrilous jests of the atheists of the time of the Revolution have gone out of vogue. But the present is characterized by refined indifference. This arises partly from the influence of that philosophy which affirms we can know nothing of God, even if He exist; but more from the peculiar emphasis laid upon the material side of life through the achievements of a marvellous civilization.

But, whatever the outward attitude, it remains true that there is no question that is more actual and more imperative than the one relating to the existence and influence of Deity. Men have sought for God from the beginning, and will to the end. With varying definitions, it has been asserted in every country and in every age, that man could hold communion with God. Mysticism, which has been defined as " the consciousness of the Infinite." has marked every epoch in religious development. Moses " saw God face to face " in the ancient days. In modern times the metaphysician declares the same truth when he writes, " The highest fact in man can hold immediate intercourse with the highest fact in the universe." The Oriental mystic speaks of the necessity of the " light in the heart which, when the sun has set, and the moon has set, and all sounds are hushed, still illumines man." While the political economist,[1] in a practical age, gives as the conclusion of his remarkable experience, " Human life is inadequate to satisfy human aspirations."

Every great faith has originated in mysticism, or " heart religion," and by it, lives. When the sense of God's constant presence is absent, religion sinks to superstition, or is smothered in

[1] John Stuart Mill.

ceremonialism. For every age, but especially the present, Heine's jest embodies a truth, "Poor old Lampe, the servant, must have his God, or there will be no happiness for him." We are so constituted that, in the natural working of our faculties, we arrive at the conception of God. The duty of the age and the church is to clarify that notion, and convert it into a practical force.

The greatest need of our time is to cultivate the consciousness of the Infinite, to leave for a time the consideration of the " beggarly elements " of the physical world, and undertake the study of human nature. We need to re-create the spirit of devotion which moves at the centre of the soul, where " illusion," if not " impossible," as the saint says, is less certain. When the church had hampered itself with useless legal restrictions, and sacrificed communion to commerce, faith to ceremonialism, associations were formed which called themselves " Friends of God." They did not break with the church, they often belonged to opposing parties; but they were one in the effort to strengthen each other in daily intercourse with God. There can be no higher duty, no deeper need, than for Christians

to-day to encourage each other in a daily walk
with God. The test of all true religion, the
measure of one's usefulness and attainment in
the Christian life, is found in the effective realization of the Divine Presence.

Walking daily with God does not involve a
miracle, but simply an awakened brain and heart.
It does not require a journey somewhere, but life
here and now. "I go," said the dying Plotinus,
"to bear the divine within me to the divine in
the universe." To die was totally unnecessary.
The divine was as near the living as the dead
Platonist. To wait for the dissolution of the
flesh, or the unveiling of a new sense, was unnecessary.

We walk with God when we look upon nature,
as did St. Bernard, as "the shadow of God" and
"the soul as his image." The earth, with its
beauty and order, is not the result of a "fortui-
tous concourse of atoms," not even the product of
"vibrating ether." It is the act of an intelligent
creation. It is not chance nor fate that moves
the wheel of life, but the hand of God. Civilization is not the outcome of an accidental train
of circumstances, but the product of a divine

mind. The material world, human history, personal life, would be impossible without the ever present and active God. Many fail to dwell upon the divine side of nature. They know nothing, think of nothing, beyond what they see. This lonely world is all in all to them, — its mountains and plains, its rivers and oceans, its sunrises and sunsets, its myriad mysteries, its gorgeous colors, its beautiful forms and sounds, its buildings, its arts, its friendships, its patriotisms, comprise all there is of life. They only see the outer beauty; its inner and divine significance is lost. "Prosperity, struggle, sadness, — it is all the same. They rejoice, they struggle, through it all alone; and when old age comes, and the companions of early days are gone, they feel that they are solitary. In all this strange, deep world, they never meet but for a moment the spirit of it who stands at their very side." But whatever the position of the believer or unbeliever, it may be said, in the words of a well-known writer, "Age after age passes; though foolish theologians and blinded atheists may wrangle with their eyes turned away from the light, the world goes on to larger and larger knowledge in spite of them, and does not lose its faith for all these darkeners of counsel may say. As in the roaring loom of time the endless web of events is woven, each strand shall make more and more clearly visible the living garment of God."

As we find God in nature, so we may walk with him as we mark the progress of events. In all great social movements, in revolutions which have altered phases of human life, quickened the sense of public honor, enlarged the freedom and enlightenment of the people, there is something more than the human element. A wise and thoughtful man will trace along the pathway of nations which have reached great exaltation the footprints of Deity. None can read the history of the progress of the world without perceiving an orderly advance, and a constant adjustment of means to ends which argues the existence of a Supreme Mind.

So we may walk with God in the hours of private and public worship, when the deepest affections and moral qualities are awakened, and spring up toward the light. Great thoughts, noble consecrations, holy aspirations, are the evidence of

the living God, are indeed God in manifestation.
To feel the constant influence of Deity, to walk
with Him hour by hour in affliction as well as
in joy, in days of weakness as well as days of
strength, in times of failure as well as success,
is to realize the true end of the Christian life,
and solve the problem of existence. Power, such
as we can never measure, and whose growth is
without limit; peace that brings a holy calm
into a heart torn by conflicting claims, and makes
" music at midnight," — are the outcome of this
attitude toward the Creator and Governor of the
universe.

But many are asking to-day, How may this
condition of mind and heart be brought about?
The answer is not difficult. The analogies of
education, illustrations from history, instances
from biography, — all point the way. First, there
must be an act of the will. Quiescence is not
the gate of inspiration. Quietism contains a
sublime truth; but when it seeks to paralyze
the motive part of our nature, it is false in
theory and practice. The method of Christ is
to " knock," " ask," and " seek." We must
be completely filled by a divine longing, but we

must work for its gratification. The world may
be full of sunshine and warmth, but if we do
not draw the shades and open the windows,
there might as well be no light and heat. The
majestic Father walks the earth in glory, smiles
at us from the face of the cloud, and throws into
our lap the prodigal gifts of love. But if we
will not open our eyes, or hold out our arms,
how shall we receive the gifts? An energetic
will drives out evil thoughts, cleanses the ways
of the mind and heart, that the Spirit may enter.
When once it feels the touch of the divine, it
cries in a kind of masterfulness, "I will not let
thee go till thou bless me." The passive mood
in religion has gone. The active mood has come.
Self-surrender to God is the highest expression
of religion. But it is possible and permanent
only as the moral nature wills and persists in
willing.

Association also plays an important part in
God-culture. When a painter would absorb the
inspiration of his guild, and prepare himself for
great achievement, he enters the company of his
fellow-workers. He places himself under the instruction of great masters. · He frequents studios

and galleries of art. Sometimes he abandons his home, and crosses leagues of ocean, to join the company of those who think of nothing, who dream of nothing, who labor for nothing, but art. So is it among scientists or would-be scientists. So is it also in the less exalted fields of trade and pleasure.

It must therefore be the same in the realm of the spirit. There must be active pursuit of God in the company of those who are engaged in the same great quest. Here, in part, is the explanation of the value of worship and meetings of devotion. We feel the magnetism of many hearts filled with the same interests and the same purposes.

Biography has an important office in revealing God, since it makes our living and personal friends and inspirers those from whom we are separated by time and circumstance. Our reading provokes our imagination to create a world which we people with the faithful or the unfaithful. Mental associates, the men and the women who come to us in apparent solitude, often exercise a tyrannous power over us. The dead speak to us in their printed word, which has unmeasured influence. Although we shun the presence of the godless in the embodied world, we are constantly under the dominance of the atheism of the invisible. So by the same law we can fill our solitary hour, our library and chamber, with the pure and lofty spirits who have believed much, and achieved much for God and man. In the spiritual economy Christ is the open door to God. He reveals God to man, is His "express image." We walk with God when we walk with Christ. Jesus is divine sonship completely realized. He is God translated into human terms, the prophecy of oneness with God which all men are to attain. In hours of strength Christ presents difficult but divine objects of endeavor. In moments of humility he exalts us by revealing our kinship to the Infinite Father. In the presence of joy he makes known the divine beneficence, and under the power of sorrow discloses the merciful discipline of Deity.

When once we give ourselves intelligently, lovingly, and with decision of will, to Christ, we shall walk daily with God. Then in nature, history, human experience, in every civilization and in every revelation, we shall find the Divine Spirit, "potent to slack the thirst of human nature, to lift eyes dim with tears and dull with pain towards the beatific vision, to heal and strengthen feet, sore and weary from the rough ways of earth, for the ascent of heaven."

THE BLESSEDNESS OF FAITH.

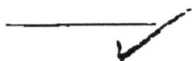

SULLIVAN HOLMAN M'COLLESTER.

THE BLESSEDNESS OF FAITH.

Our little girl of two summers, as she was sitting on the grassy lawn, picking clover blossoms, saying, as she held them up to her mother, "beautiful," was giving an expression to an intuition of beauty, not to an idea which she had learned. When the child of six years old was asked by the philosopher, "how she knows there is a God?" answered, "My think tells me so," the sage could not gainsay the reply. As the physician inquired of the convalescent youth, "how she knew that she had a soul?" responded, "My consciousness, or feeling, tells me so." — "Ah!" continued the doctor, "did you ever see it?" — "No." — "Did you ever hear it?" — "No." — "Did you ever taste it?" — "No." — "Did you ever smell it?" — "No." — "Did you ever feel it?" — "Yes." — "Then," continued the wise man, "you have only one sense in favor, and four against it." She retorted, "Doctor, do

you know there is any such thing as pain?"—
"Yes, I think I do, when I have the jumping
toothache," was his reply.—"Well," she continued, "did you ever see it, taste it, smell it,
hear it?"—"No, but I have felt it."—"So you
have four senses against it, and only one in its
favor." Thus it is in the higher conditions of
living,—life itself is not only the foundation
of knowledge, but certain knowledge inheres in
it. Often it does not require demonstration, as
in mathematics to prove that the three angles
of a triangle are equal to two right angles, but
somehow it possesses the truth, or the knowledge
of the facts. This is a gift, not an acquirement;
it is inherent, not an accretion. Thus the belief in God and immortality is born with men.
Our deepest convictions are not the outcome
of logic; they are higher than the grasp of
reason. This is particularly true of our religious
convictions.

We are wont to say that the poet and musi-
cian are born. Culture alone could not produce
a Whittier, or a Beethoven, because it is impossible for a lower to create a higher. The order
is God, angel, man, beast, bird, fish, insect, mi-

crobe. So we can understand why all things good are possible with God; and why we have different orders, conditions, and administrations; and why souls should have insight by a special gift to things higher than themselves. Now, this insight and outsight is faith, or soul-sight; it is the soul's going out of itself for what it craves. ·This is what sees God and friends. I know we are apt to talk as though it were far otherwise. We often magnify the body to the belittlement of the soul. We are accustomed to speak of burying a friend, when we place his mortality in the grave, just as though a hundred and fifty pounds of matter constituted the man.

The fact is, we do not recognize one another through the flesh. The child comes to know its mother only as heart touches heart, mind communes with mind, and the spiritual takes cognizance of the spiritual. The body to-day is not what it was yesterday; it is incessantly changing; it can be divided into parts, and its particles are being constantly displaced; its life can ·be but a span long. But the soul is a unit; its faculties cannot be separated; they are bound into an everlasting oneness, enabling man to see and know the spiritual, to love and admire what is unseen to the natural eye.

It is true there are those who honestly say, they cannot believe, only so far as they can touch, handle, and reason out things. There are those who can make no headway in geometry or classic literature; this does not prove that these are not facts, it only shows mental defectiveness, or a want of certain intellectual perception. This lack may have resulted from heredity or home education. Therefore, when one says he cannot believe, that he has no faith in any hereafter, that at death he shall drop into nonentity, he is to be pitied. One without any esthetic perception, or musical appreciation, is to be commiserated, but nothing so much as he who has no spiritual insight.

As we read the doubts of Diderot, Hume, Shelley, and John Stuart Mill, they do not make us feel as though life were worth living. An insect with its eyes destroyed buzzes and dodges around strangely; so it is with men without faith; they beat themselves wofully against the wall, till at length their flesh falls into the dust. Sense pierces into the deformities of things, and finds them evanescent; while faith penetrates beneath and beyond the seen, to the unfailing and real.

So faith is an attribute of the soul, made up of trust, confidence, and courage, which sees, as the setting sun throws back the colors of gold and rubies, a bright to-morrow; it has clearest vision of the future. Experience unfolds past ages, and faith penetrates the realms of futurity; it is nothing else but the soul's venture. As the farmer sows his seed, faith shows him the harvest. As the mariner loses sight of the port left, his faith exhibits the haven towards which his steamer is sailing; by the showing of astronomy, we come to know that the sun is ninety-five millions of miles distant from the earth; through this quality of soul, or mind, we are enabled to see, as science speaks, that the lightest of gases is a mineral, that there are minerals which swim on the water and take fire at the touch of snow, that the diamond is but a bit of melted charcoal, and that pearls are only the resultant of disease. Were it not for this attribute of the mind, the mother, as she kisses her darling, could not see him a noble man; the teacher, in listening to the recitation of a precocious student, would

not discover him a philosopher in the unfolding
years, neither would that boy have dared leap
from the fourth story of a building on fire, as
he heard his father's voice ascending through the
lurid smoke, saying, "Leap, my son, I am here
to catch you." Faith exhibited to him, in spite
of raging flames and blackest clouds, his father;
and he leaped, and was caught in paternal arms,
rescued from a terrible death. It was such sight
that enabled the old man, taking the Christ-child
in his arms, and raising his eyes to heaven, to
say, "Now lettest thou thy servant depart in
peace." Surely the believing soul at the foot
of the cross can see a risen Christ.

This quality of character too seldom receives
full recognition. It is prone to be treated as
something mystical or fanciful, or at least not
more than half certain. We are not wont to
examine sufficiently, to ascertain the fact that we
begin to think in the realm of faith; that we trust
friends before we know them, and in ourselves before we comprehend our individuality; that really
it is a force which underlies consciousness and
throws open the door to knowledge. It is true
that it is less liable to misapprehension in common

affairs than the spiritual. The man of business could not get on at all, did he not feel the potency of this soul-force, giving him sight of what is ahead. It enables him to look through a day, a month, or years, perceiving possible riches; and then with what will he dares the wolves in the way, and struggles for the entity near, or far off. From height to height he pushes on for the golden pitcher filled with the silver waters. As blossoms are before the fruitage, so is faith before good works.

Faith embodies trust, confidence, and courage; so the adventurer, listening to tales of rivers running over golden sands, like the ancient Pactolus, leaves, and ventures all to gain wondrous treasures. The sick man, hearing of sunny climes and invigorating lands, bids adieu to home, and travels far off to reach his anticipated goal. Faith is really the fashioner of all great souls. Had it not been for it, Abraham never would have found the Promised Land; Columbus never could have endured the raging of the ocean and the contumely of his crew in searching for the new world; Washington would have deserted his charge in the time of the Revolution, when shamefully taunted and

thwarted in his noblest endeavors; Sir Walter
Scott would have found no peace and power to
write his last thrilling stories under the burden of
heavy debts which had been unjustly thrust upon
him. All great souls have been subject to trying
disappointments, and have triumphed because of
faith. Therefore Jesus sorrowed as no others,
and yet he gained the greatest victories. As faith
brings to light the invisible, it fills the soul with
patience and courage. It discovers God not only
everywhere, but all of God at every point, not
his wisdom here and his goodness there, not his
love to-day and his justice yesterday; but he is
the same personality always and in every place.

Faith is the soul's eye, through which we see
God or man. It is only when filmed that it cannot endure the light. Still one, while in the flesh,
who sees a distant result, seldom knows just how
it is to be attained; for this reason, when he is
making a worthy pilgrimage, his tent is certain to
be pitched on higher ground than he anticipated,
however, never above the peak his soul sighted.
Accordingly, Savonarola could witness the dawning of a new day, when priests were lurking in
shadows and stirring up fagots to burn muscle

and bone which never see, thinking thereby to
destroy the dauntless seer. Christ knew, when
the blind Pharisees were driving the nails into his
limbs and thrusting the spear into his side, that
he himself was not being crucified, that only mortal garments were being torn off that his spirit
might go free. He well understood that space
and time, flesh and blood, have no belonging to
the soul's realm ; so he could declare, without a
guess or venture, 'If this outward body of mine
be destroyed, I shall come to you within three
days, because I am the resurrection.' In fulfilment of this promise, the Marys were greeted by
him on that first Sunday morning that ever was,
as they came to the tomb where his body had
been laid. Peter and John, and the sojourners at
Emmaus, were made inexpressibly glad as he appeared to them. They felt in duty bound to
declare at once what they had seen, that the rest
of the apostles and disciples might rejoice with
them ; and as they were assembled for this purpose in a private room, who should put in his
presence but Jesus himself, upbraiding them for
their slowness of belief, or want of faith. To
Thomas matter was more real than mind, hence

he was not going to admit the resurrection true until he had put his fingers into the prints of the nails and the spear. The visible was more real to him than the invisible, the same as it had been to the Israelites, and especially to the Egyptians, who had built vast pyramids and cut into solid rock immense tombs for preserving the bodies of kings and honored men. But in the course of forty days from the crucifixion, all the apostles came to recognize Christ out of the flesh. After this insight and outsight were developed, what far-seeing men the chosen twelve became! There was no more denying nor doubting on their part. They had now come to realize that men know one another only as they see soul to soul, — a fact which men have been slow to understand, though illustrated by daily experience in all the past. Without this faith-sight there can be no sweet home, no true friendship in the school, or cordial fellowship in the church. The descent of the Holy Spirit is naught but the mind's sighting God, the means through which we see the Father. In these latter days we have been hearing much about faith-missions, faith-healing, faith-science, and faith-works, and all these have more or less significance when fairly treated, and can be accounted for only on the ground of faith, which is just as real as the law of gravitation; the first pertains to spirit, the latter to matter. They both work by invariable laws of their own. Faith is the vital principle of the spiritual life, just as much as breathing is the vital sustainer of the body; and the flesh can exist just as well without pure air as the spirit without faith. This is the soul's Rock of Ages, on which it can stand, however terrific the storm or raging the flood.

The following statements of Christ are in perfect accord with this line of thought: "And he said unto her, Daughter, thy faith hath made thee whole; go in peace, and be whole of thy plague."

"And he said unto him, Arise, go thy way: thy faith hath made thee whole."

"And he said to the woman, Thy faith hath saved thee; go in peace."

"Then touched he their eyes saying, According to your faith be it unto you."

"Again Jesus said unto him, If thou canst believe, all things are possible unto him that believeth."

We understand that all good things are possible

unto God, and here Jesus informs us that all things unto men are possible so far as they can believe. So then our study should be to discover the law by which faith works. Then experiment with it as much as we may, it does seem to be no more nor less than clear-sightedness of God, or any good which is revealed through trust and confidence.

When the first Christian martyr was led out of Jerusalem, and placed upon the projecting ledge, and the young Saul stood there, holding the garments of the ruffians as they hurled the missiles of death at Saint Stephen, looking straight into heaven, he saw the glory of God, and prayed, "lay not this sin to their charge," and then fell physically asleep, or, in other words, was translated. His sight of God was so clear as to render him sufficiently strong to return good for evil. No doubt that Saul was surprised at such a glorified departure; and as he was sent forth not long after by the august Sanhedrim to demolish the little church, established in the name of Christ at Damascus, it is not strange, as he walked the paths made memorable by the beneficent deeds of Jesus, that he should have been so wrought upon as to have had his spiritual eye cleared in a manner to allow him to see Christ distinctly, whom he never had seen in the flesh. By this experience he was so transformed as to enter Damascus to bless all, and henceforth to love all men. This was no other than Paul, the scholar, who became the greatest of the apostles, enabling him to send forth the refrain, "Thanks be to God, who giveth us the victory through our Lord Jesus Christ."

We can well understand how an artist can feed his mind so much on the skill and life of his master as to become like him, and so follow close in his footsteps. Thus it was with Leonardo da Vinci, as his great teacher, when becoming feeble and unable to complete his last work, requested da Vinci to finish it. At first the apprentice felt that it would be impossible for him to attempt to put the finishing touches to a picture of his revered master, so skilled and exalted; but as his beloved senior bid him do his best, he first knelt in prayer, asking, "O Lord, help me in my weakness, that I may do faithful service to my deserving teacher, who has done so much for me." Upon this he took his brush, and became lost in doing his best; and after the finishing touch had been given it, the aged and cultured artist was brought into the studio on a litter, and as he looked upon the great work, in tears of joy he said, "I paint no more."

Thus Paul caught such views of Christ in the spiritual life that he could but assert in most emphatic terms, "Now is Christ risen from the dead, and become the first-fruits of them that slept; for if in this life only we have hope in Christ, we are of all men most miserable. As in Adam all die, even so in Christ shall all be made alive. For he is to reign till he hath put all enemies under his feet. As we have borne the image of the earthy, so we shall bear the image of the heavenly." Thus he declares that "faith is the evidence of things not seen " with the natural eye. Faith *is* the soul's eye to discover things invisible to the physical sight. For this reason, he says, "We now see through a glass darkly, but then we shall see face to face." In other words, in looking through mortal sight, we behold constant change and mystery; but seeing spiritually, we recognize God and our departed, as having personality. Such visions so filled the heart of Paul that he most emphatically declared, "Here

we know in part, but then shall we know as we
are known." To him there was no such thing
as ceasing to be, or lying dormant in the grave.
The only possible death is moral death, the result
of sinning. But as none *can earn* eternal life, so
none *can deserve* eternal death. The apostle sets
this matter clear when he affirms, "As a man sows,
so shall he reap." Who could thoughtfully wish
to have it otherwise? Just recompense is what
encourages righteousness and restrains wrong-
ness. Paul makes death the gate which opens
from the mortal to the immortal. He allows
no dark angels to hover around it, but seraphs
of light, to usher souls into eternal life. "Even
so in Christ all are made alive."

This was the experience of that band of Christian women at the time of great persecution in
France, as they were being led through the streets
of Paris to the place of execution, enabling them
to sweetly sing, "Lord Jesus, we come, we come."
As they reached the block the lookers-on felt they
had never heard such music before; and the melt-
ing strains did not cease as head after head fell
to the ground, till the last one dropped from the
block. Here faith did its perfect work.

It is sad that the Christian world has been so reluctant in learning what is the true nature of faith. Too often it would seem that efforts have been made to render it obscure by belaboring it with theological definitions. Many apparently have been anxious to hang on its tree foreign fruit, yet striving to make it appear as though natural, which has been as inconsistent as it would be for an orchardist to buy apples, and hang them on his trees to secure a good crop. Fruit must grow, never be tied on; this is the law of all kinds of fruit-growing.

None can honestly question the need of faith. I exist, and I am conscious that I did not create myself, and had nothing to do or say about coming into this world; therefore I know that some one higher than myself fashioned me, whom I call God. Now, faith in Him I need above all else, for by it I gain knowledge of him. Our senses tell us how things look, taste, smell, feel, and sound. Reason explains their relations, and how causes are certain to be followed by effects. Now, must there not be something beyond these? If I do not believe there is, I am wretched indeed. Modern investigation shows the boundaries of science and philosophy. Astronomy can take us only to the stars, not beyond them. Geology turns up the stony leaves of the earth, but cannot read to us a page of the how and why it exists. The entomologist, as he brings his glass to bear upon a drop of water, revealing myriads of moving mites, can give us no explanation of their vital force, or how they came to live. Now, where science and philosophy end, faith begins; and whosoever fails to be led on by its potency, falls prostrate at the first hill of the spiritual, and there he is likely to lie in the swamp and filth of agnosticism. Take your grandchild upon your knee, as some friend calls, and as his attention is directed to the bright boy, suppose he begins at once to expatiate about the boy's dress, stockings, shoes, and hair, saying not a word really about the child, that expresses so much through the eye, laugh, and gesture; how would you like that treatment, and what would you say of it? Suppose the visitor should declare that all these peculiarities signify naught. Would you not feel inclined to apply to him the epithet, "a know-nothing"? When invited into a German studio where a young sculptor was moulding an ideal statue of Abraham Lincoln in 1866, what if I had simply spoken of his plaster, trowel, and room, without expressing any admiration of the statue and its naturalness; would the gifted artist have thought me *compos mentis?* He could see so much beneath the exterior, he would have had reason at least to wonder why the stranger did not discover some of the real things which he was trying so hard to delineate. He might truthfully have said, the foreigner has evidently no mental eye, or vision of faith, whereby to discover the ideal and intrinsic. The author of Hebrews says, " By faith we understand that the worlds have been formed by the word of God, so that what is seen hath not been made out of things which do appear." Notice how he puts it, " By faith we understand." Accordingly, he regarded faith as something that comprehends, does actually see and understand.

This view of faith was beautifully illustrated by Cecil's little daughter. One day, as she was happily playing with some inferior beads and other trinkets, the father said, " My child, please throw all those objects you have in your hands into the fire." Startled as she was, she looked

up into her father's face to see if he were really
in earnest, when he continued, "You know, my
child, I never request you to do anything which
I do not mean; still, you can act your pleasure,
obey or disobey, yet you know I never wish
you to do any act. which I do not feel will
work for your good in the end." Upon this
the precious one sighed, but, mustering up courage, she cast all these keepsakes into the flames.
Upon this the father said, "There, let them
vanish; you shall hear more about them hereafter." In the course of a few days the father
came into his house with a whole box of play-
things, larger and handsomer than the burned,
and placed them in the hands of the daughter,
saying, "These are yours, because you believed
and trusted me, when I told you to throw away
those inferior trifles. Now, by thus doing, you
have gained these far more valuable keepsakes.
Furthermore, I ask you always to remember that
that working of your mind and heart which induced you to obey me is faith. Now, I would
have you always do towards God, in his provi-
dential dealings with you, as you have with me,
and you will be a true child of faith." In this

we see that her spirit of filial love overcame every other emotion or impulse, causing her to act altogether with reference to the unseen, thereby illustrating what faith is, and how it works. So, if we act towards God as this child did towards her father, we shall portray true faith, realizing in the end thrilling gladness and gratitude.

In this age physical science is exceedingly fascinating. The botanist, as he analyzes plant and flower; the geologist, as he studies pebble and bowlder; the astronomer, as he explores planet and star; and the anatomist, as he dissects nerve and muscle, — often become so charmed with their specialities, as to infer that there can be nothing superior to them. As such attempt to account for organized life, it is usually on the ground that molecules chance to come together, and this will explain its origin; or others assume that it has sprung from minute cells and eggs floating in the sap and blood, — and yet they have failed to tell whence came the first plant to produce the cell, or the first bird to lay the egg.

Now, away with all such pretentious learning,

and, like the child, bow before the superior, and we shall soon be taught how mind is more than matter, and spirit than flesh; that soul-sight is real sight; and so be made to understand that it is God who rounds the apple, and carves the pear, and paints them scarlet and russet; that it is God who lifts up the oak from the acorn; that it is God who raises up the tiny child into noble manhood; that it is God who, in spring-time, when the fields look bare and lifeless, lets fall the April sunshine and showers, and in the course of a few weeks spreads a carpet of emerald over the fields and woods; that it is God who has caused the sixty different elements so to combine as to produce an infinitude of worlds, and chained them together by gravitation.

It is by faith that we understand who made all things good. Then, is it not needed? Try to account for the merest object without this help, and how we are staggered and soon floored. By it we discover how the higher is helping the lower; the vegetable is moulding the mineral, the human the animal; we come to realize that God is the cause of all this. As we examine and compare, we see how there is similarity of lives. The bee constructs its comb, the fox its burrow, the bird its nest, and man his dwelling, that all may have homes. Faith informs us that the how and why of this is God. He has filled the normal state of existence with fulness of joy; for this reason the bug ticks in the wall, the cricket chirps in the grass, the frog whistles in the pool, the bird sings in the tree-top, and the little child laughs and sports on the lawn.

Still, in spite of this similarity, there are un-likenesses. Man can reason, and do somewhat as he pleases; but insect and beast must do as they are bidden. Faith sees that this is for the best. Without this gift, or quality of soul, blindness, perplexity, discouragement, and weari-ness of life would fret and discourage mortals. Faith keeps lifting up and pressing on, and whenever reason falters, it flies ahead and in-vites it on. When the latter anxiously asks, "Is man to live forever?" the former opens wide the gate, and lets fall upon it the radiance of heaven. Now, as the latter applies its logic, it discovers how the mortal reaches perfection here; but man falls far short of it, so its conclusion is that man must continue to live beyond the physical. Then, as it discovers the adaptation of things, how the bird has wings and air has been made for their use; how fish have fins and water has been provided for them, — thus again it infers, as these wants are met, that, since man desires above all else to live forever, he must be gratified, and elsewhere than in this world.

For the most part, faith takes up the work here and carries it on, making it plain why the flowers bloom, and so soon fade away; why the rainbow arches the sky with glowing promise, and then so quickly disappears; why myriads of shells radiate their beauty in the depths of the sea, with no eye to admire their charms. These disappear without having any dirge sung, because they were made for this world. But it is far otherwise with the child, the mature, and the old, as they go hence. We learn patience by long endurance; we sow in tears that we may reap in joy, for the reason we were not made to finish our course here; we barely gain the foot of the everlasting mountain; we only get down to the beach of the great ocean of life. But the eye of faith descries the endless hereafter and scans an eternal future, rendering immortality a reality. Is not such a ken demanded?

All this, and vastly more, exhibits the blessedness of faith. It tempers the whole soul and fuses it with truest fortitude. If poverty oppresses, dangers threaten, and sickness is unto death, it penetrates beyond the veil and runs for the goal. It makes life signify, not simply happiness, but development. How blessed the revealment that man is always to grow! Naught can surpass this fact and help so much while he is tabernacled in the flesh; without it he groans and wearies of existence.

When in the metropolitan church of Copenhagen, I was delighted with Thorwaldsen's statue of Christ. Probably it is the most perfect representation of the Divine One ever made by human genius and skill. Long did the great sculptor enthusiastically and intently work upon it; but when it was at last finished, it is said that a deep sadness came over him, and, when asked the reason, his reply was: " My genius is failing me. Here is my statue of Christ; it is the first of my works with which I have ever been satisfied. Till now my ideal has always been far beyond what I

could execute ; but it is no longer so. I shall
never have a great idea again." Yes, to feel that
we have attained to the pinnacle, and that we are
to go no higher, is heart-crushing.

But one under the exercise of devout Christian
faith never suffers any such abrading disappointment. Abraham left his native city, Ur, though
he loved it dearly, and went with his aged sire to
Haran to dwell, for he felt that he would have a
better opportunity to grow; and after he had tenderly cared for his aged father and seen him
through this life, then he journeyed far away to
Canaan, suffering severest hardships for the sake
of worshipping unmolested the one living God.
So he led his beloved Isaac to the mountain-top,
and was ready to offer him a sacrifice unto God,
for he was made to believe that would prove the
best for his son and himself. He was especially
guided by faith.

The greatest human deeds have been done by
men of faith. It was through the blessedness of
faith that the Pilgrim Fathers settled this country ;
that Livingstone opened up the heart of Africa ;
that Xavier bore the cross of Christ to India. This
it was that sustained Galileo, Newton, Faraday,

and Herschel in their researches. This gave unfailing courage to Paul and Peter, Luther and
Murray. These were the glad servants of the
Most High, whom they had come to know through
faith. Thus conditioned, every true soul has gone
out of this life glorified. Is this not true of Mary,
who broke the vase of ointment and poured it on
her Lord? She did the best she could, and her
doing has lived as a memorial unto her through
the centuries. The old artist in Paris, whose faith
had led him into his garret out of sight of the
world to mould a likeness of Christ, was building
the best he could. As night came, and with it
chilling frosts, the old man lay down to sleep. At
midnight he was awakened by the freezing blast,
and he arose, taking off his coat and coverlet,
laid them carefully over his statue lest it might
freeze, and then laid himself again on his pallet of
straw. When the morning came a friend opened
the door of the destitute studio, and lo, the statue
was complete and safe, but its designer and exec-
utor was cold in death; he had given himself
for his work. What a resplendent crown of blessedness rests upon his life! The young Confed-
erate soldier at the battle of Fredericksburg, after

a bloody contest, heard groans and entreaties for water all through the night; and as the dawning came he said to his general : " I cannot stand such beseeching any longer, and I am going to carry water to those poor suffering fellows." His commander said, " It will be death to you, if you attempt any such rashness." The reply was, " I have faith to believe that the Lord will not let the Union soldiers fire upon me in being merciful unto their wounded comrades." For an hour and a half he was distributing water to parched lips, and laying weary heads in the most comfortable position possible, and no harm befell him. Really, he must have experienced more solid happiness in that brief time than he would have realized in ordinary life during years of well-doing. So it is, faith renders the soul daring for the right, which is sure to be followed with great recompense.

It is related of a young girl who manifested uncommon loveliness of character, that she wore around her neck a chain with a locket attached to it, which she did not allow any one to open. But she was taken sick, and it would seem unto death ; and as one of her intimate companions

was watching by her, she was permitted to open
the keepsake, and there was found in it this writ-
ing : " Whom not having seen, I love." Herein
was revealed the secret of her purity. Faith in
Christ had transfigured her life, and filled her
soul with blessedness. This is the agency alone
that can perfect human life.

Nothing is sadder than to walk among incomplete ruins. Perchance there were good begin-
nings, but from uncalled-for reasons no finishing
was given them. Thus it is with the young man
who starts out from the old home full of promise,
leaving expectant hearts behind, and enters a city
career, paying more deference to outside show
than to principle. In a few years his faults ex-
pose him, and he falls ruined. The man who
sacrifices his all for the sake of riches, that he
may count his millions before the world, never
using his means to improve society and make
others wiser and happier, falls sooner or later
amidst incomplete ruins. The sceptic who delights in tearing down, but proffers no substitute,
never completes any work ; and, however long he
lives, he finally falls under a mass of ruins. If one
be born a philosopher, and by force of education

is made a doubter and disbeliever in God and man, he never departs leaving a completed pile; his shafts are broken and his foundations are sand. His only monument left is built out of the sand of remorse and wretchedness.

Perchance there would be no mass of physical ruins at old Babylon, Palmyra, or Athens, had it not been first for the materialization of human character, and the obliterating of moral responsibility. Wherever affections have become fixed on things sensual, rendering spiritual progress impossible, obliteration has always sooner or later come to such men. The history of paganism, or atheism, is but one vast volume, delineating human ruins. They are sure to be changed to violence in their action. With such men it is rumors of war, and wars continually. Edmund Burke estimates that such have destroyed upon the field of battle more than thirty thousand millions of human lives. They have influenced human legislators to enact cruel penalties. Paganism has represented God revengeful above all other intelligences, rescuing the few and destroying the many. Barbarian philosophy has pictured countless and unending ruins. A faith-

less man is a failure, just as much as a steam-
engine would be without fire or boiler.

But the men of Christian faith have builded
for the ages. Christ has been the chiefest of all
in the greatest works. As he walked amidst the
shadows of time, he exhibited the splendors of
eternity. He loved the lilies and stars as the Father's handiwork. He took little children in his
arms and blessed them, and stimulated the mature to highest endeavors. Faith did its perfect
work in him, making his whole life redolent with
blessedness. He gathered up what goodness he
could from Confucian morality, from Brahminism
in its grasp for the real, from Buddhism in its
search for virtue, from Zoroastrianism in its eager-
ness for more light, from the beautiful in Athens,
and the law of Rome. He came not to destroy
the dispensation of Moses, nor the songs of David,
but to fill them full of the love of God. He
so combined the good of the past, the present,
and future, as to form a perfect doctrine. He
breathed the good of all the world into his gospel. He built Christianity upon the blessedness
of faith, infusing it with immortal vigor. This
is the realization of a soul baptized into the pro-

foundest faith. This makes it ready to hear what
God has to speak, and do what he wills to be
done. So his surrender is unconditional, ready
to go whither duty bids, to bear any burden
imposed, to make any sacrifice, however costly,
hoping all things, and pressing towards his lof-
tiest ideal. He incessantly struggles at his edifice of character, if he does not know whether it
is to be finished according to his plan, or not,
believing that it will go on to completion in the
building not made with hands. He cannot discover room enough in to-day for the blessings
which he sights in to-morrow. Thus his own
uncertainty results in the certainty of God. Ultimate failure, disaster, and destruction are impossible to him.

The superlative blessedness of faith is, that it
makes God the beginning of all good things. It
sees him unfolding all souls in his tender embrace, loving, chastening, and training, that they
may develop as rapidly as possible from lower
to higher orders. It writes " beautiful " over
every tomb, setting ajar its door, where angels
stand, sending out the consoling refrain, " He
is not here, but is risen."

LOVE AS AN INNER FORCE.

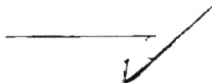

FRANK WARREN WHIPPEN.

LOVE AS AN INNER FORCE.

A DEFINITION of love is as difficult to make as a definition of soul. We can describe love. We can see many of its component parts. But the aggregate of these parts leaves us far short of the whole. We can never define the supreme grace.

In our common use of the word love, it has many objects. Men are said to love good and also evil, things and persons, one soul, a family, and a race. There is little in common between love of money and love of a friend, and a pity it is that the same word should stand for both. We crave names sacredly to be kept for the deep and holy things. If love is to stand for the supreme affection of souls, other words should tell of the lower passions.

There is some reason, however, in letting the word run over the wide scale. There is a common factor. In each case the passion or the affection is a motive. Every state of the soul which we are inclined to call love has its effect as a powerful inner force.

We see this true of the love of money. Men do everything for gain. Charity, friendship, honor, decency, and respect for the sacredness of life itself, are all set aside in the face of that mighty passion. No wonder the truth has been magnified into the proverb, "The love of money is the root of all evil." All people have felt the motive. Idolatry, in many forms, has been local, and in the course of ages has passed away; but here is an idolatry that seems to have begun with the beginning, and now, at the very close of the nineteenth century of the Christian era, shows little signs of ending. Men, not a few, love money now better than they love their next of kin, and better than they love righteousness or their God, — and this love is the mainspring of their lives.

We turn gladly to more hopeful things, and one is the love of country. Here is a motive we can honor. This makes men brave and devoted. Our hearts are thrilled by the deeds of the patriots. They take us to the eternal things. It

is so with Arnold Winkelried, as he throws himself onto the Austrian line, to make a way for
the Swiss, and receives into his body a hundred
spears. It is so with the Pilgrim Fathers, when,
though exiled by the English king, they dare
the stormy Atlantic and the wilderness in order
to plant a colony for that king, because they love
England so much. It is so with Washington
and Lincoln, as they struggle on in the face of
the greatest difficulties, in behalf of liberty and
human rights and national union.

All the patriots move us. The rehearsal of
their devotion makes us more devoted. Our
own national heroes are a part of our inheritance,
and our emotion is as pure as the thoughts of
angels, and powerful in the direction of good
citizenship, when our hearts in song echo the
sentiment of the poet's words : —

> " Thy name I love ;
> I love thy rocks and rills,
> Thy woods and templed hills ;
> My heart with rapture thrills,
> Like that above."

Another form of this inner force is the love
of nature. The result in this case may not be

so striking as in many others, but it is as real. Among those elements in men's lives that may be said to run as undercurrents, few mean more than does a loving intimacy with the great world around us. He who loves nature has a set of motives which other souls lack. He is led by them out into her realm. He is made to see values which figures are powerless to express. In the woods, on the hills, by the rivers, the lakes, and the sea, he finds treasures, which any other of like spirit may also find, which are treasures indeed because they feed the soul. The love of nature banishes wantonness, and quickens the humanities. Souls blessed with it are moved to respect even the humblest life. Frank Bolles pauses to regret that he has unwittingly disturbed an ant-hill; and such as he are reluctant to tread down even the tiniest flower. Justice and sympathy are born of this spirit, and they reach to all the affairs of men.

Plainly, love of any sort is a force. What we love we are interested in, and have an enthusiasm for; and wherever there is interest and enthusiasm there is motive. And yet, there is a love that is pre-eminently strong, and in the motive that it supplies, supreme above all others. If love is "the highest word," this is the kind of love that exclusively may claim the name. Even the most tender affections must be passed by to see it in its completeness.

It is more than the love between man and woman. And this is mighty. What will the lover not do for his beloved! What will frail woman not endure and give up that she may have the companionship which her heart craves! There is little extravagance in Shakespeare's lines : —

> " O, gentle Proteus, Love's a mighty Lord:
>   And hath so humbled me, as, I confess,
>   There is no woe to his correction,
>   Nor to his service, no such joy on earth."

But the supreme love is more than this. And to reach it we must pass by even the love of mothers. No love can be intenser than a mother's. All that soul can do for soul a mother will do for her child. Comforts she will forego, pride she will stifle, danger she will dare, starvation and death she will endure, for her child. Eliza, the slave-woman, whom Harriet Beecher Stowe has immortalized in story, leaping with her boy in her arms onto the floating ice of the Ohio, and passing desperately from one cake to another with bare and bleeding feet, but in safety, to the northern shore, is the heroic type of what this kind of love will prompt. No hardship or risk that can be named, whether it be of a moment or of a lifetime, is too great for a mother's heart.

The supreme love may not be intenser than such, but it is supreme even over the love of mothers, because it is far-reaching. The supreme love overleaps the bounds of maternal love, and goes out to man as man, and out to God. When we talk about love as Christ talked about it, this is the love we mean. All other love is secondary, along the way it may be, to that warmth and sympathy of heart which directs itself to all humanity. This love is the divinely appointed bond, not simply between two souls, or a few, but between the souls of the race. Love is the recognition of the universal brotherhood. It is the realization of the common Creator and the common blood of men.

Love in a sense is before righteousness. The world was a sinful world, but God loved it so

that he sent his Son to save it. Jesus loved sin-
ners, and there is the secret of his power over
them. So, in men, love does not vary with character. Love takes note of character. It takes
keener note of it than any other power. But
it lives, and ofttimes sublimely, in spite of the
worst in souls.

Evil, it is true, cannot be loved with the love
that we speak of now. The Devil, were there
such a person, a person totally and hopelessly
committed to evil, could not be loved. Love is
a divine grace. Only those beings that have
something of the divine within them, either actual or potential, can be loved. But love can
embrace wicked men, because in them there are
godlike possibilities.

Love is the ideal attitude of one soul toward
all other souls. Nothing in earth or heaven can
cancel it. The affection of a parent clinging to
an erring child, sacrificing for him, patiently enduring for him, leading him home when he has
so far lost himself that he must be led, following him to prison and to the gallows, and saying
through it all, " He is my son," and ceasing
never for a moment to yearn for him and love

him, — the affection of such a parent, as far as quality is concerned, is the type of that love to which Christ has called the world; and which, present in the soul, is life, the eternal life of God.

Love, then, is a temper of soul. It is an inner grace. You cannot see it or take note of it by any of the senses. Its immediate results are all within. Longing, yearning, and ecstasy are words that tell its power. It is a solace and a peace to those that have it. At the still hour it is a blessing.

But love is more than a temper of soul, more than an affection to be shut up and enjoyed, and so profited by. Love is an inner force. Present in souls, it moves them to deeds. Jesus said as much to Peter in that last conversation by the lakeside. Peter claimed to love his Master. Doubtless he did love him; and yet, but a few days before, he had denied him three times, and, with the rest of the disciples, when the critical hour came, he had forsaken him and fled. Jesus says nothing about this now, but he teaches his lesson, nevertheless. Most impressively he couples two ideas that Peter, doubtless, had never before felt to be so close. Three times his Master asks him if he loves him. And to the answer, "yes," repeated with increasing emphasis, he responds each time substantially in the same words, "Feed my sheep." Peter said, "I love." Jesus answered, "Serve, then. If you love me, be good and generous and helpful to me, or what amounts to the same thing, to your fellowmen." It seems as though Jesus would have Peter tell him, in answer to his question, not simply "yes," but as a far more significant answer, "Lord, I am going out to carry your message, and the forgiveness and peace which you have brought to me, to the world that needs so much. Lord, I love you, and to attest that love I am going to be your disciple in deed and in truth." This, at least, is what the reply of Jesus means. If Peter really loved him, he must do so. If he loved, his love must move him, it must be a force in him operative for the good which love must wish for men.

And so, by this principle that love is an inner force, that, present in souls, it will in one way or another make itself felt, we have a test of love. No man need be in doubt as to whether the divine grace is his. If it is his to any marked degree, he will know it by what it makes him do. He cannot love much, and do nothing, or little. He cannot love, and shut himself up away from men. And he who finds himself so shut up, who has no generous impulses toward others, who is not impelled to deeds of mercy and helpfulness, no matter what his professions, or where his name is written, — he is as poor as the poorest, in the riches of the Master's kingdom.

What, now, can love do? To little Paul Dombey's question, "What can money do?" his father replied, "Money, Paul, can do anything." But even Dombey Senior, in response to Paul's persistent questioning, was obliged to admit limitations to the power of money. Money could not stay the hand of death, as it reached out for Mr. Dombey's wife, and it could not make little Paul a strong and robust boy. Mr. Dombey admitted this, but still his faith in the power of money remained unshaken. He did not recognize that in certain situations, where it is trusted very much, money is completely without avail; that it cannot bring contentment, or joy, or peace; that the richest may be miserable with his wealth.

But the answer which Dickens puts into the

mouth of Mr. Dombey is suggestive. Before the realization that money cannot do everything, we are prompted to ask, Is there anything powerful to such a degree? Can we substitute any word for money in Mr. Dombey's statement, and let the statement stand? In one sense we cannot; with man some things are impossible. As it was with little Paul's dear mamma, and his own frailty itself, so it always is. The flame of our mortality will grow feeble, and flicker, and go out. And yet, in another sense, we can substitute a word for Mr. Dombey's money, and make his statement profoundly true. When we substitute the word love, we do this. Making allowance for the limitations necessary to man, love can do anything.

It is wonderful in its power to make hearts glad. What sunlight is upon this earth and in our homes, love is in our hearts. It is the secret of spiritual health. We live through the influences of love. Where love is there is security from life's trials. As in the deep sea, so here,—

" There is a temple sacred evermore,
  And all the babble of life's angry voices
  Dies in hushed stillness at its peaceful door."

Love is our support in solitude. No matter
how far away from men we are, if we love, we
are one with them in spirit. The tie can bridge
the gulf of death. We grieve to be parted from
our loved ones, but because we love them we can
follow them on, and know them ours still. The
love in our hearts, quickened by Christ, is the
secret of our victory over death and the grave.
So we can look into the face of our dear dead,
and still thank God.

This great sympathy can make one glad, too,
in the society of strangers. There is no feeling
of loneliness greater than that which comes over
one in a crowd. The situation is sometimes like
being at sea without water. Just as in such a
case there is " water everywhere, and not a drop
to drink," so in the crowd there are faces all
about, but none with greetings. Such surroundings may chill a soul like death, but they need
not. A loving heart will find greetings. Faces
will not seem cold or indifferent to him who
really loves humanity. Though seeing them for
the first time, he reads in them the universal
traits. He sees in them trials and sorrows, hopes
and joys; and the pity and sympathy of his heart

leave no room for loneliness. Such a soul will turn strangers into friends.

Men have devised other plans for doing the same thing. The Masonic order and kindred organizations have this for a part of their object. By their mystic signs welcome is assured in strange cities and distant lands. This welcome is no doubt realized. And·yet, in the long run, love is at the foundation even of this reception. The warm, generous hearts find the true friends even in the fraternities. Love opens every door. It is the universal passport.

Love in the heart is a source of gladness because loving is living. Love means spiritual health. Even sorrow and great trials do not cancel all life's gladness in the loving soul. Love never lets a soul come to that point where life seems not worth the living. On the other hand, it prompts continually to the thought, "How good it is to be!" We have a kindred feeling on those rare days God gives us, when physical beauty and the winsomeness of nature in earth and air and sky are forced upon us. What we call the perfect days fill our souls, and so this love of God and of man, filling men's souls, prompts them to cheerfulness and peace. Thank God for the perfect days, and for the peace of the perfect grace.

Thank God, too, for the activity of the perfect grace. Love can do well-nigh everything. It can influence souls for good. Men will listen to those who love them, those whose interest in them is genuine and sincere. Love is the secret of success in the great reforms. The human heart is reached by sympathy. Men demur at being treated simply as cases. They respond only feebly to mechanical appeals. Many things can be done by machinery, but saving souls is not one of these. Men are influenced for good by sympathy. Soul after soul has gone to the bad, and souls are still in that way, because no kind word has ever been spoken to them, and no hand, expressive of a warm heart, has grasped theirs to make them feel the universal bond. What pathos in the response of an abandoned soul when surprised by kindness, "No human being ever spoke a kind word to me or put a hand on me in any mood but hate and scorn before!" —- what pathos and what hope!

Love saves. It is well to call things by their right names. We hear and read a great deal in these days about the missionary spirit, and we should. All churches are trying to cultivate that spirit, and this is well. But this one truth we cannot for a moment afford to lose sight of, that the missionary spirit, in the missionary himself and in those who send him, is not an artificial and abnormal thing, but at its heart this divine grace. Love is the missionary spirit. Love makes workers successful among the wayward, the abandoned, and the ignorant; and just in proportion to their love of humanity will churches have this much-talked-of grace.

In the teacher love is worth more than brains. He may command, but he cannot inspire without it. One of the greatest elements of strength, and at the same time one of the profoundest needs in our public schools to-day, is men and women with hearts. Only by sympathy can teachers appreciate the needs or the capacities of their pupils. Only by loving familiarity with them can they impress them with the truth. Love gets behind the mere teaching of facts to their meaning. Without their meaning facts are well-nigh useless. The school-teacher wields a sceptre for good second to no other, if his heart beats warm and true.

And with love is the solution of the social and economic questions that vex us. And there is no other solution. The great evil is, men do not love each other, do not feel the common bond. They are indifferent, selfish, cruel. They are separated into factions, and each looks upon the other with no sympathy. Eighteen hundred years and more ago the doctrine of the unity of the race was set forth, and men have not accepted it yet. Remedies for existing evils there may be in legislation and in other devices, but the cure depends upon the softening of men's stony hearts. Men must think of each other, especially of people below them, " as if they were fellow-passengers to the grave, and not another race of creatures bound on other journeys." Love vanishes oppression on the one hand and envy on the other, and insures the true relation between men.

It is the province of love also to promote righteousness. Love and unrighteousness do not accord. The heart warm with sympathy does no wrong to others, and at the same time is anxious that others shall be true. Dr. Livingstone had comparatively little trouble with the natives

in the wilds of Africa. William Penn was re-
spected and trusted by the American Indians,
because he was kind to them, and because he
treated them as brothers, and few men in history have a nobler record than his.

It is said sometimes to reformers, " These
things are not your business, you are meddling ;
take care of yourselves, and we will do the
same." But the charge is made in error. A
real interest in humanity cannot be content with
wickedness. It is the business of love to seek
to better the world, and to lessen the evil and
the sorrow of it.

Love chords only with the virtues. Those we
love we want to be pure and good and true.
There are many names applied by the lover, but
the supreme of these is "angel." Parents wish
various things for their children, but the supreme wish runs out in the direction of character. Love in the hearts of fathers and mothers
makes them desire above all things else that their
boys and girls grow up manly and womanly.

Love toward humanity may not be as intense as
the lover's or the mother's, but in effect it must be
the same. As a mother weeps over her straying

boy, and as Jesus wept over Jerusalem, so hearts with love in them must sorrow before the wrong.

And love must not only sorrow, but act. Love says, when confronted with a sadly erring soul, " I will try and help him. The weight is heavy on the side of sin; I will throw all the influence I can bring upon the other side." Love always says this, for " love rejoiceth not in iniquity, but rejoiceth in the truth."

Love shows itself an inner force when we think of self-sacrifice. Deny yourselves, Jesus repeatedly said to his followers. And we cannot wonder that they failed to understand him, and that they disobeyed in this even in the most solemn hours. We can see how his followers later made their mistake and crucified their bodies, with the thought of thereby saving their souls and serving their Lord. The doctrine of self-giving rises grim and stern from every point but one. There all harshness is done away, and the light of heaven is on it. That point is love. In love is the motive. Denying one's self for the sake of denial is a stoical and profitless act. But denying one's self in order thereby to help another is grand. Suffering pain as an exercise is folly;

but suffering pain in another's stead, or for another's welfare, is blessed satisfaction. Such sacrifice is reasonable and natural. It is of the very essence of love to say, " Let me suffer for him." In love the apparent inconsistency between Jesus' call, " sacrifice yourselves," and the angel's message, " I bring you good tidings of great joy," is done away. Where love rules there is joy in giving one's self for others.

Love is a bond of union where other things tend to keep souls apart. It is the ground upon which all differences sink away. Men may believe opposites, and yet be·one in sympathy ; they may have the prejudice of a life-time cancelled by the all-conquering grace. Stronger than prejudice was the aversion between Jew and Samaritan. Each was bred to hate the other. And yet love could overflow such hate. The Jew left for dead on the road to Jericho found a Samaritan's help. In spite of inherited hate, the Samaritan had a heart. He was willing to help even a Jew, and giving up to him his own beast, take his chances with him on a robber-infested road.

And although times have changed, the Good Samaritan is a character as full of beauty to-day as he was in the days of Jesus. Society is divided into factions now, as of old, and the church is divided. In religion men do not think alike or see alike. It does not appear that they ever will. But for that reason they need not be at variance. It is not creeds that keep the churches apart, so much as it is lack of knowledge one of another, and a spirit that comes very near a spirit of partisanship, and, above all, a lack of the loving spirit of their common Lord.

This is where we should expect the trouble. We are called to live with the spirit of Christ in our hearts. Because we lack this spirit, we are cold and distant to the church people over the way. The receipt for Christian unity is growth in the divine grace. Souls moved by love will never turn contemptuously from any sincere soul, but will be ready and eager to give him the cordial hand.

Love fails sometimes, but it fails because it is alloyed, because it is mixed with other things. Perfect love is the perfect motive. It is the motive of God, the motive of Christ, the motive to be sought and prayed for, and treasured and rejoiced in; the motive that shall take the race on to the complete victory.

THE RICHES OF THE SCRIPTURES.

Edward Lovell Houghton.

THE RICHES OF THE SCRIPTURES.

THE chief object of this essay is not to prove
that the Bible is a collection of inspired books in
this or that sense, nor even that it is inspired at
all. It is not to champion this or that view of the
origin, authorship, and date of the several books.
It is simply to take these books for what they are
in themselves, as books which have sufficiently
proved, by the spiritual experience of centuries,
that they have spiritual profit in them; and to
offer some suggestions as to how the greatest
possible measure of such profit may be realized
for the needs of present every-day life.

Questions of criticism have their own interest
and importance. The practical significance of
such questions, in their bearing upon the value
of the Scriptures for spiritual profit, may easily
be over-estimated, — often has been, very greatly.
By way of illustration, take two examples.

Some critics say the Pentateuch was written,

or rather put into its present form, in the time of Josiah; others, not until after the return from the Babylonian captivity. It is evidently a composite work, based upon several documents of widely different dates. Very well; what of it? Those critics whose opinions differ most from traditional views, although they do not say so as explicitly as might be desired, still admit that the substantial basis of the Pentateuch is made up of genuine history and genuine usages of the Mosaic epoch and earlier. The work of the later writers of these successive periods was, for the most part, simply that of editors. The Pentateuch, as we have it, is substantially correct history of the Mosaic and preceding epochs. The prophetic writings and the older Psalms may be older than the present *form* of the Pentateuch, as many critics, perhaps the majority, to-day hold, but have by no means yet been able to prove. To maintain that these writings would have been possible except on the foundation of the *substantial contents* of the Pentateuch, inwrought into the thought and life of the Hebrew people, would be like trying to balance a pyramid on its apex. The practical value of these or of any Old Tes-

tament books for present spiritual profit is not
affected one particle by modern critical theories.

For another example, take the Fourth Gospel.
Recent discoveries, particularly the most recent,
that of the ancient Harmony of Tatian, may well
be said to have rendered the opinion that this
Gospel is a second-century document entirely
antiquated, and to have settled it beyond question that it is the work of the Apostle John
(with the exception, of course, of chap. xxi.).
But suppose it were otherwise. Suppose it were
a second-century document. The book is still
what it is in itself; incomparably the deepest,
fullest, most sympathetic presentation of the life
and character of Jesus we have. The truthful-
ness of the picture is self-evident. No writer,
even of the apostolic age, much less of that following, could have invented it. It must have
been drawn from the life. None could have
overdrawn it. It is simply a question of different degrees of apprehension, all partial, by different disciples of the Great Teacher. None of
them, do his very best, could do more than present a partial picture of a figure too majestic to
be fully comprehended. The real Christ must

have been far greater than the most exalted picture we possess of him. John lived a much longer life, hence had more time for reflection, and a deeper and richer Christian experience than his fellow-disciples. He could apprehend, hence could remember and relate, many of the deeper things of his Master's teaching which they did not understand, and so forgot. This it is which makes the Christ of the Fourth Gospel so much greater than the same personage as the other evangelists present him to us. Not that the picture in the Fourth Gospel is overdrawn — that would be impossible; but this writer gives a view which is nearer to the reality, the reality itself being still far beyond this or any possible portrayal. It is this quality which makes the Fourth Gospel the richest, the most valuable for spiritual profit, of all the biographies of Jesus. And this is equally true, whenever and by whomsoever written.

Taking the Bible, then, for what it is in itself, without regard, except incidentally and in very subordinate degree, to critical questions of date and authorship, without regard to the question of its inspiration, except as its divine character may appear from the internal evidence of its own contents, let us ask how this book may be used so as to yield the greatest possible degree of practical spiritual benefit. The Bible has nourished the spiritual life of many thousands for many centuries. The same spiritual needs exist under the changed conditions of modern life. How may the Bible be made to minister most fruitfully to those needs?

1. *Point of view.* — Scripture is not all alike, nor all of equal value, particularly not for purposes of spiritual profit. Furthermore, it does not follow, because certain Scripture is not suitable for use in a certain way, that it may not have large value when used in another, the right way.

An especially broad distinction exists, and therefore should be made, between the Old Testament and the New. Not only should a broad distinction be made, but the right one. It is important not only to avoid the formerly more prevalent mistake of regarding the whole Bible, Old Testament as well as New, as the one perfect moral and spiritual guide for all time; it is even more important to guard against the opposite error, now far more common, that the New Testament alone has any present spiritual value, the Old Testament being altogether antiquated and valueless.

The moral standard of the Old Testament is manifestly imperfect. It is folly to attempt to deny that fact; very unfortunate to fail to realize it fully, and the significance of it. Does it mean that the Old Testament has no divine element in it, and no present spiritual value? Or is there a point of view, thereby proved to be the right one, from which, in spite of its imperfections, yes, in part even by means of them, both the divine element and the power of spiritual instruction may be clearly seen?

One of the prophets has what comes very near being an explicit statement of such a point of view. God is represented as saying (Hos. xi. 3), "I taught Ephraim to go, taking them by the arms." Ephraim is the Hebrew people, of whose history, laws, customs, political fortunes, religious aspirations, and apostasies the Old Testament is a partial record. The figure is that of a mother teaching her child to walk, taking it by the arms, and thus guiding and supporting its

first feeble, tottering steps, until it is able to go
alone. God says his procedure with the Hebrew
people has been like that of a mother training
her child. Does not the figure fit the facts?

Suppose we take our stand at Mount Sinai.
We shall thus be led directly to the consideration
of the chief defects of the Old Covenant, therefore
to the chief obstacle in the way of the traditional
view of the equal value and perfection of all
Scripture. It may be that we shall find in these
very things, when looked at from the right point
of view, even deeper lessons of divine wisdom
and love than could possibly have been obtained
under the former view. Here is the Hebrew
people, ignorant, childish, passionate, stiff-necked,
just released from centuries of hard bondage.
This people is to be trained to become the centre of moral and religious light for all the world.
A tremendous task, worthy indeed of divine
power, if not beyond even that! Now, upon
sound human principles of education, how may
the divine wisdom be expected to attack such a
problem as this? For principles which are really
sound as human principles are also sound as divine principles.

It is a cardinal principle of all successful education not to attempt to teach everything at once; to teach first those things which are most fundamental and necessary, and to adapt the teaching always to the capacity of the pupil. Even the perfect wisdom and power of God must be limited, in the moral and spiritual education of his children, by their capacity. Even he cannot at once do as he would, but must do as he can.

Applying these principles to the task of the moral education of a childish people like the Hebrews, we should expect that the moral code first proclaimed to such a people would be direct and specific. It will not be a single principle of life, nor a set of principles, leaving the people to work out and apply them for themselves. Such a procedure belongs to a more advanced stage of moral education. It is not adapted to the beginning. It will say to them, Thou shalt do this, and Thou shalt not do that, of a considerable number of specific outward acts. Is not this an accurate description of the Mosaic legislation?

We should expect, secondly, that the list of specific things thus prohibited would by no means include everything now considered clearly wrong under an advanced Christian civilization. It is probable, rather, that the worst, most fundamental, most destructive sins will be fixed upon — those most absolutely fatal to the life of the nation and to its success in its mission. These will be prohibited absolutely, under the most stringent penalties. Other things, to us as clearly wrong as any prohibited, but not so fatal to the life of the nation or to its fitness for its mission, might be treated in the partial way next to be referred to, or even entirely ignored.

We should expect, in the third place, that many evil things which were not so vitally related to the existence and mission of the nation, which, moreover, were matters of deeply seated custom, and therefore could not be made to seem wrong to them as they do to us, would be not prohibited, but hedged about with restrictions designed to lessen their evil results — leaving their absolute prohibition as sins to be the work of the greater moral enlightenment to come later.

In the light of these two last-mentioned principles of wise moral education, let us look once again at the Old Testament legislation, both as to what it forbids and as to the way it treats evil things which it does not forbid. There are two sins against which the whole Old Testament is especially severe — the worship of false gods and impurity. Bearing in mind the mission of this people to be the centre of religious light for the world, the wisdom of such a course is manifest. The two sins were closely related. Impurity was associated with, a part of, the religious rites of the nations round about the Hebrews. They themselves were especially prone to it. No sin is so destructive to a people's usefulness and even existence as this. A pure worship and a pure life this nation must preserve; else it could not succeed in its mission. And, although only after many falls, they at last learned the lesson; and when Christ came with the new, perfect law which was to supersede the old, imperfect one, he found a people who, though marred by many faults and grave, were yet remarkably pure in worship and life, and that in an age of unexampled profligacy.

On the other hand, the Old Testament legislalation does not forbid human slavery. It was a common custom, and recognized as such in the law. But note how the institution is surrounded by beneficent checks. The slave must refrain from labor on the Sabbath as much as his master. If a Hebrew, he must be treated rather as a hired servant than a slave, and at the end of six years must be set free again. The position of foreign slaves was less favorable; but if a master murdered his slave, he was punished with death the same as if he had killed a freeman. If he destroyed his eye, or struck out a tooth, the slave must be given his liberty. A very different institution this from other ancient slavery, — equally so from most modern.

Polygamy was also a common custom of the time. It would have been impossible to make the Hebrews see that it was wrong. The time was not ripe to prohibit it altogether. So the law contented itself with prohibiting certain improper marriages, and limiting the loose divorce practices of other nations, whereby the husband might dismiss his wife at pleasure, not, indeed, to the extent of the Christian law, yet so as materially to diminish the evils of the common custom.

The custom of blood-vengeance, by which it was looked upon as the duty of the nearest relative of a murdered man to pursue and slay his

murderer, was, and still is, very firmly fixed in
the Oriental mind, as in some other people's. To
eradicate it would have been impossible. Hence
the institution of the six cities of refuge in different parts of the land, to which the slayer might
flee from the avenger of blood, and there be safe
until he could have a fair trial.

The law provided that, in certain cases, the
rulers might even stone to death a stubborn child.
We should regard such an act as murder, and
rightly. But when we reflect that the common
custom and thought of the time gave a father
absolute power of life and death over his household, this provision, with its safeguards, takes on
a very different, a positively beneficent, aspect.

These illustrations will sufficiently justify the
position before taken, that there is a point of
view, thereby proved to be the right one, from
which, in spite of its imperfections, in part even
because of them, both the divine element and the
power of spiritual instruction in the Old Testament may be clearly seen. This point of view is
that of the education of a morally imperfect,
childish people to be the centre of religious light
for the world. Moral teaching meant for such

a people will necessarily, hence rightly, be imperfect. It is not to be judged by its intrinsic
contents, like the Christian teaching, but by its
tendency. We are to accept nothing, as a practical guide for present life, which falls below the
highest standard of the Christian consciousness,
enlightened to the utmost by the highest teaching
of the Christian law, interpreted by the best
Christian experience. Yet these older Scriptures,
when viewed from this standpoint, will be found
to contain spiritual riches scarcely inferior to the
New Testament itself.

They are valuable as history. All history is
pervaded by the divine presence, and is full of
spiritual teaching for those who have the open eye
to see it, but no other to such an extent as that
of the Hebrew people. They are particularly
valuable as the self-evident record of the particular dealings of God, the great Teacher, with a
particular people, intended for a mission wholly
different from that of any other. Looked at from
the vantage-ground of these Christian centuries,
and from the true point of view, the wisdom and
love of the Heavenly Father shine out scarcely
less when, far back in the dim ages of antiquity,

he condescended to the weakness, the imperfection, the hardness of heart, of his wayward children, and took the best means, imperfect and rude and severe as they oftentimes were, to teach them the first fundamental lessons which they must learn, in order to be fitted for their great mission to the world, — scarcely less manifest, *to us*, are his wisdom and love in these preparatory stages of man's moral education, when, like a mother teaching her child to walk, he taught Ephraim to go, taking them by the arms, than in the final and perfect stage of God manifest in the life and teachings of Jesus Christ.

That life and its teachings are the height and centre of all the Scriptures. Judge all, as to contents, by this standard. But let it not be forgotten that not all, perhaps not the chief part, of the spiritual value of many Scriptures is in their direct teaching. This ought often to be utterly rejected, while the very same writings may have very great spiritual riches, to be seen only from the right standpoint. All before the Christ is preparatory; all after, the working out, more or less perfectly, of what is in his teachings. The point of view is all important, that the real riches of all the Scriptures, both Old and New, may be found, and turned to the greatest possible spiritual profit.

2. *Topical Study.* — Beside the reading of favorite passages in the Bible for devotion, for comfort, for spiritual sustenance, which has been a common practice all through the Christian ages, a more or less systematic *topical* study will be found to yield very great spiritual profit. The plan of reading the Bible through in course, so many chapters a day, leaves much to be desired, especially in the Old Testament. The attentive reader will not fail to gather many pearls even thus; but there is a more profitable way to spend what time one has to give to study of the Scriptures. Aside from the more ambitious topical analyses, of which there are many, even the busy reader, who can have at the most but a brief time for such study, may use the topical method to some extent and with much profit. In your reading you come to a view of God's providence, of man's nature, duty, or destiny, of sin, temptation, forgiveness, which arrests your attention. A natural question is, Just what does the writer mean? What does he say elsewhere on the same subject? What do

other biblical writers say about it? The Scriptures have a vocabulary of considerable extent
and striking power, which is peculiar to themselves and the literature founded upon them. To
grasp fully the meaning of these peculiarly Christian words and phrases is to understand Christianity itself; to fail to do so is to be certain not to
understand it. What does Jesus mean by eternal
life, the day of judgment, the kingdom of God?
What does Paul mean by justification, the flesh,
the spirit, faith, works, grace? Commentators
will give you their opinion. That may be good
and helpful. It is better that you make up your
own opinion by topical study of the writer himself, which, indeed, in the main, is the very way
in which the commentators made up theirs. The
marginal references to be found in many Bibles
will help you. Any good concordance will help
you. The more elaborate topical analyses will
help you still more if you can have more time
for study. And the more you study the Scriptures in this way the greater the spiritual riches
they will unfold to you.

3. *Biographical Study.* — Let the Bible be
looked upon as a book, not of dogma, but **of**

life, — not even of life in the abstract, but of particular, actual human lives. Religion has lost nearly all its possible value when it is regarded as solely or chiefly a system of impersonal institutions, laws, and doctrines. The Christian religion has its great doctrines indeed, but they are doctrines *alive*, working in the living hearts of living men. It can be of value to us or to any one only as it comes into our lives, and with living power uplifts and transforms them. Nothing will conduce so much to this result, which is the spiritual profit for which the Scriptures are designed, as to study them in this way — not as mere doctrine, but as doctrine engaged in its proper work of moulding the character of one and another living man. Study the Scriptures as books of biography. Let the characters found there be real, living men and women.

If we regard and study the biblical books and characters in this way, it will speedily be borne in upon us, how very modern, after all, is this old Book — or, rather, how independent of all ages — in its essentials ! The outward details of expression, manner, custom, are often strange, sometimes even grotesque, to our thought. But underneath all this is the same human nature, weak, imperfect, yet godlike, suffering, sorrowing, sinning and repenting, loving, as at present. And there is the same Heavenly Father guiding, blessing, reproving, training his children; in each age adapting his teaching to their capacity with the same unerring wisdom shown in later times. The lives of these ancient worthies, — and unworthies too, — the mouthpieces, and objects, and instruments, just as in different ways men and women of later times have been, of that divine grace and wisdom which are unchanging and eternal, may be means of great spiritual profit to us.

Study the character of Abraham. Note the effect it had upon him to be called, in whatever way, from the midst of a nation of idolaters, and made the possessor of the great truth that God is one. See how this great idea, coming to that man away back in the dim ages of the past, in the fresh force of its newness, wrought upon his mind. To us this idea is matter of inheritance. Let us put ourselves, so far as possible, in the place of one to whom it came for the first time, as a new thing, and its living power over ourselves cannot fail to be greatly increased.

Study Moses, the great leader and lawgiver of Israel. His was one of the master-minds of the world. No critic makes him a myth, or essentially alters the main facts of his life and character.

Study Elijah, the earnest and fiery prophet of God. Behold him as he rebukes the wicked king and queen of Israel, or as he stands, the sole prophet of the Most High, before the four hundred prophets of a false god. Correct, if you will, what is savage and imperfect in him by the example of Jesus when facing the representatives of evil under somewhat similar circumstances, and then let the ancient prophet teach you a lesson of moral courage. It is a lesson as much needed in these times of peace and luxury and secret corruption, as in those of violence and open profligacy.

Let Achan impress with the fateful progress from gazing upon the evil thing to coveting, then to sin and its awful consequences. Let Balaam warn us against the fatal infatuation for material gain which makes deaf to the commands of duty, and blind to the inevitable triumph of God and righteousness.

The life of David will have many lessons for us, — some of the highest uplifting power, in which he will seem to raise us almost to the Christian level; some of the most solemn warning, when he descends to the depths of the grossest sins; again, and perhaps the most valuable of all, in his equally deep repentance, and in the inevitable retribution which, repentance or no repentance, every sin of itself works out upon the transgressor.

Turn to the New Testament. Study John the Baptist, the humble forerunner of the Christ, of whom he said, " Among those that are born of women there hath not arisen a greater than John the Baptist." Note his utter humility and faithfulness to his own comparatively lowly mission in the face of temptation to assume a higher. " Art thou the Christ? No. Art thou Elijah? No. Art thou the prophet? No. Who then art thou? I am the voice of one crying in the wilderness, Prepare ye the way of the Lord." To his disciples, over-zealous for his honor, on which the rising fame of the new teacher seemed to them to be encroaching, he said, " He must increase, but I must decrease." Yet there was, with the humility, a courage and fiery zeal for duty which could face the severest test without flinching, — whether it be the arrogance of the corrupt Pharisees, or the anger of an abandoned queen, bringing with it the prison and the headsman's block.

Read Paul, not for the doctrine alone, but to see the man behind the doctrine. Make him a companion, a familiar one. Let him speak to you as he did to the Romans, to the Corinthians, to the Philippians, to Timothy. Let his great personality, shining out through his writings, have its natural effect upon you. It cannot fail to be uplifting and spiritually profitable. John, the beloved disciple, whose long life and ripe Christian experience enabled him at last to give us a higher, fuller, more sympathetic view of his Master than any one else, is valuable to us not only for that, but also for himself, to teach us by the power of his own personality that spirit of love which he set forth so clearly as the central principle of Christianity.

Peter, the impetuous disciple, James, the apostle of common sense, Stephen, the first martyr, beside many others of whom we know less, may be made productive of much spiritual profit, especially when studied not only for what they teach in word, but as living men, like ourselves, worked upon by the same gospel, living, under human conditions, with human excellences and human imperfections, the life of service of the same Master.

Above all, study the life and character of the Christ himself. A marked difference will soon make itself manifest. All the others, great men, very great though some of them were, were yet evidently altogether men like ourselves, and fully comprehensible. Here we are conscious of something beyond our comprehension. In all the others weaknesses and imperfections could be discovered; some were guilty of flagrant and open sin; the chief lesson to be derived from some of them was one of warning. Here all is purity and perfection. Jesus is perfectly human, and yet there is nothing human about him in the sense in which we often use the word, as implying weakness, imperfection, sin. He is not such as we actually are; but he is what we ought to be, what we have the possibility of being, what we are destined to become. Notwithstanding the fact that he is so far above our present powers of comprehension, indeed precisely because of it, he is our supreme model.

There is no possibility of fabrication here. There were none then, there never have been any, competent to such a task. The fabricator of such a character as that of Jesus would be more wonderful than Jesus himself.

Then let the Christ be a real and living personality to you. Let the Christ himself look at you, speak to you, live before you, die in your sight. Join the band of his disciples, and go in their company and his over the mountains of Judea, across the lake of Galilee, to Capernaum and Sychar and Jerusalem. Walk with him through the fields, and let him unfold his parables to you. Sit at his feet as he speaks the Sermon on the Mount; stand with the woman by the well in Samaria, and let him teach you as he taught her; go with him and the two disciples on the walk to Emmaus. Follow him to the wedding in Cana; to the temple enclosure, where he contends with scribe and Pharisee; to the tomb of Lazarus; and finally to Gethsemane and Calvary. Such intimacy with the matchless personality of Jesus cannot fail to bring rich spiritual profit — far richer than the study, however diligent, of the mere letter of his teachings.

4. *Helps.* — Helps are good, but there is need of discretion, both as to numbers and manner of use. Over-many helps and commentaries are ofttimes like burying one's self in the midst of a mountain forest, when what is really wanted is an unobstructed view from the summit. One will often feel the need of returning to the Scripture itself to refresh its own direct impression upon the mind, and to recover from the feeling of confusion very likely to be the result of reading many differing, perhaps conflicting, views *about* the Scripture. Use helps, so far as they are helps. They may suggest to you many a thought of spiritual profit which might otherwise escape your attention. But never let them deprive you of your own judgment as to the inner meaning of any passage you are studying. Helps used for the purpose of obviating the necessity of doing your own thinking and using your own judgment are not helps, but hindrances, to obtaining spiritual benefit from the Scriptures. Nor let outside helps overshadow the best of all interpreters of the Bible, which is the Bible itself.

Excellent helps in scriptural study, available for all, are such as a good Teacher's Bible, with its marginal references and other helpful matter; a good concordance; such works as Geikie's *Hours with the Bible*, for the Old Testament, his *Life of Christ*, and Conybeare and Howson's *St. Paul*, for the New. These works are not controversial, nor mainly critical, but helpful; and a knowledge of the original tongues is not necessary in order to make large use of them.

Use the Revised Version. It often leaves something to be desired in felicity of expression as compared with the old version; but its painstaking accuracy resolves many a perplexity, and brings out here and there not a little of beauty and suggestiveness which would never occur to a reader of the old. For examples, see Ps. lxxxiv. 5, 6; John iv. 27: [his disciples] marvelled that he talked with the woman (old version) — quite colorless and devoid of suggestion; they marvelled that he was speaking with a woman (Revised Version) — a change of the article only, yet immediately suggestive of the Oriental idea that it was unsuitable for men to hold converse with women upon high themes, or indeed any conversation at all except the briefest possible upon the most commonplace and necessary matters; and secondarily, of the wonderful change in the position and treatment of women wrought in the world by the power of the teaching and example of him who, so many centuries ago, sat wearied by the well in Samaria, and gave the water of life freely, just exactly as he did to men, to this sinful, but thirsty-souled woman. Similar cases, where the Revised Version resolves some perplexity of the old, or throws some new light upon the Scripture, are to be found on almost every page, especially numerous, perhaps, in the Psalms and Pauline Epistles.

Such reading and study of the Scriptures cannot fail to reveal ever greater spiritual riches in them. One must not commit the old error of expecting to find, in all parts of the extensive and varied library of sacred books which we bind together and call the Bible, equal measure of spiritual value. Nor must he fall into the opposite error of supposing that parts of it which have been superseded in their direct teaching by the coming of later and higher revelations, may not still have very large spiritual value when viewed from the right standpoint, and used in the right way. The point of view is all-important.

Let the study be often topical, so as to yield a comprehensive view of what the whole Scriptures teach on this or that matter respecting God, his character and relation to his children, and man's nature, duty, and destiny. Let it be often biographical, that so, beholding the divine teachings of the Scriptures working themselves out in actual human lives, these teachings may have more of living power, and so of spiritual profit, for our own lives. Make use of all good helps, but do not overestimate their value, nor allow them to overshadow the best of all interpreters of the Scriptures, the Scriptures themselves.

Finally, let it not be inferred from the questioning of traditional opinions and the conflicting views of scholars upon matters of literary criticism that the spiritual value of the Scriptures is in any wise diminished, made doubtful, or greatly affected in any way. The chief part of what the Scriptures are, they are in themselves. The spiritual power of the Scriptures through the centuries past has not been dependent upon particular views of the origin and authorship of the separate books, nor is it so dependent now. Questions of literary criticism have their own interest, but only slightly, if at all, do they affect the chief value of the Scriptures, which is in their power of spiritual uplifting, instruction, suggestiveness. It is in the hope of aiding in the search for these spiritual riches of the Scriptures that the suggestions of this essay have been made.

MOULDED BY THE INVISIBLE.

CHARLES SUMNER NICKERSON.

MOULDED BY THE INVISIBLE.

WHAT is man? When that question is answered, we have determined the possibilities of human nature and the methods of moral development. Then we can prophesy with comparative accuracy, and foretell whether a human being is to be content with a vision from the level of experience and observation, or whether he, inevitably, will be dissatisfied until he looks out upon the world of life from the summit of attainment. And if he has within him innate propulsive energy, — energy which compels him forward and upward, — we can, if we understand aright the nature of that energy, be able to affirm what its propulsion can accomplish of itself, and as to whether there will be need of any supplementary agency to bring man to the condition in which he will find absolute satisfaction.

As soon as we enter upon the path of investigation we are met by those who have made a

study before us, and they begin to advise and
to admonish. It is boldly and unhesitatingly
asserted by some that man is a creature of dust;
that all we see and all we know is simply the
activity of matter. The record of Genesis, it is
affirmed, has at least one fact when it says that
man was formed of "the dust of the ground."
It may be that the dust has become highly
attenuated; that it has changed its form, and
made its appearance in new and subtile fashions.
Nevertheless, it is dust. A certain physicist says,
"I do not know of a single naturalist of any
distinction in the world who does not think and
say that all phenomena exhibited by plants and
animals are due to physical and chemical causes
alone." And he quotes another as saying that
"certain it is that life is a chemical function."

This means that we are, as persons, in every
particular, identical in primal constituent elements. Man is nothing more than the sand beneath his feet, when that sand is sufficiently "attenuated." What we are is "flesh," and "of the
earth, earthly." In the last analysis there is one
substance — matter, having at least two phases
of manifestation. A psychologist affirms that,

"Mind and body, consciousness and brain, are evolved as different forms of expression of one and the same being." "We have no right to take mind and body for two beings, *or substances* in reciprocal interaction. On the contrary, we are impelled to conceive the material interaction between the brain and nervous system as an outer form of the inner ideal unity of consciousness." "Both parallelism and proportionality between the activity of consciousness and cerebral activity point to an *identity* at bottom."

The conclusion is, therefore, that we are bodies, flesh and blood. About us there is nothing else. We are beings made up of innumerable atoms. Says a scientist, "By a body, then, we mean a local habitat for a living thing; *we also mean* the LIVING THING ITSELF."

Glad as we are to know what the naturalist thinks, we continue our research because we believe there are others just as eager for the truth as is he, others who are just as competent to inform us as is he. We do not believe that even naturalists have learned all there is to learn, or that wisdom will depart from this life with them. They have many facts, it is true; but they theorize about the facts they hold, just as do other people.

By the psychologist we are told that there is a realm of phenomena which is radically different from that to which our attention has been called. Have we not some power or powers besides those of touch, taste, sight, and smell? Is everything to us simply sense-perception? Do we know nothing otherwise? Not that we must believe with the Platonists that original ideas and first truths are known by some special sense called the " Divine Reason; " nor with the Schoolmen that those truths are discerned by " light of nature " and the " light of reason; " nor with Descartes that they are " innate in or connate with the soul; " nor with Hume and his disciples that we know them by " association." The inquiry at this point is not so much as to the acceptance of somebody's peculiar philosophy of how we know, as it is as to whether we have " knowledge " itself. Do we know other than through our senses?

The answer comes that we know ourselves as ourselves, distinct from anything else. We know that we distinguish something about ourselves as distinct, not only from the matter which consti-

tutes our environment, but as well from our own
bodies. The thing seen or heard is not the agent
which sees or hears. We are able to distinguish
our bodily organs from certain states or conditions in which we find ourselves. We resist certain bodily desires, as hunger, passion, or sleep.
The phenomena discerned by the senses are motion, color, sound, combustion, breathing, growth,
height, decomposition, and the like. These have
relation to space in that they "require extension
in the substance on which they operate, or in the
effect or activity itself." There are the phenomena, such as emotion, will, thought, memory, joy,
sorrow, purpose and resolve, remorse and repentance, of which we know just as certainly, but
which admit of no such relation to space as the
former, nor do they — even as does the electric
fluid — require a certain amount of matter to
be made living in order that they exhibit vital
activity. What, then, shall we call this power by
which we know so much, and so much that is
radically different from that which the senses
afford? Of course we must give it some appel-
lation, in order that we may speak of it, and make
less difficult the use of it. Let it be called soul.

This sounds something conscious of itself. It has a means of distinguishing itself from all else — from things about it, and from its own states and actions, as already declared. Any man who will turn his thought inward upon himself and pursue subjective study will be convinced that he is himself and not another, and that he knows immediately and directly his own joy and sorrow, his own choices or recollections. There is no logic in all the world that can force him to conclude otherwise.

It is this appeal which is to be made when we would answer the initial question, "What is man?" No one is prepared to answer judicially unless he has passed in review the claims of the materialistic naturalist and of the psychologist. Whatever claims may be made by the former as to the connection of soul with a body, its development with the body, its dependence upon the body for knowledge, or its being an ultimate form of matter, and therefore that body and soul are material organizations, the latter being simply a higher function of the former, — all such claims are met and their force overwhelmed by the fact that the phenomena of the soul are totally unlike the phenomena of the body, — not material nor requiring material substance to make known their existence; that the soul distinguishes itself from all matter with which it may come in contact, and what that distinction inevitably involves; that the soul is self-active, impelled to activity by its own energy and not of the senses which merely direct, but do not cause, that activity. Self-consciousness asserts that man is an invisible, unweighable, untouchable something, which is capable of self-direction and self-determination. He inhabits, for a season, a tenement constructed of clay, but he differs from the tenement in very many regards. While the body is the "local habitat" for a "living thing," the range of phenomena of which the "living thing" is appreciative and cognizant is so unique in every particular that the "living thing" must be pronounced as something different from the "habitat" — as something different and more than the body. And since thought, feeling, choice, joy, sorrow, memory, and resolve make up much the vaster amount of our life, we are forced to regard that "living thing" which knows of these as distinctly its own states or activities, as the chiefest, grandest, sublimest of all our constituency — as the man himself. In other words, we are compelled to the conclusion that man is a soul, a spiritual entity.

Various experiments have been made in order to discover the source of being. Whence life? has been an inquiry for ages. Not infrequently it has been asserted that the powers resident in nature were of sufficient content to account for all that we see and know. Though there be myriad of form, color, and combination, there is an efficient cause for all in natural agency. "Matter is eternal," "Nature is eternal," has been the dictum of some.

Others have said that there was and is spontaneous generation. Seekers after truth took their implements, and proceeded to determine whether this were fact. They sought for matter absolutely lifeless. That is, they endeavored, by certain processes, to destroy all life that might have existed in the matter which they had in hand. And having secured what they believed to be such material, they watched and waited with excited interest. Imagine their concern — perhaps delight — as they saw manifestations of vitality in what they had previously believed altogether devoid of

life. Was spontaneous generation a fact? Had
they solved one of the mightiest problems of all
ages? These were some of the questions of their
own minds. But being candid men, who sought
only for the truth, they reinvestigated; and, as
the result of that reinvestigation, they announced,
not an absolute disbelief in spontaneous generation, but rather that, so far as their experiments
were concerned, that theory of the origin of life
had not been substantiated.

The law of cause and effect being readily
accepted, there was no escape from the conse-
quence that, since generation was not spontaneous,
and since it was evidently an effect, either it was
caused by Nature, as has been asserted, or by an
efficient something outside of Nature. As Professor Flint and others assert, " The mind of every
thoughtful man is forced to one of these two conclusions; either that the universe is self-existent,
or that it was created by a self-existent being."

The truth, therefore, that the soul of man differs in its nature from the body and other material things, induces consideration as to what
produced it, with its peculiarities of nature and
function. Certainly it could not have come from

something entirely inferior to itself. That which is lower cannot of itself and alone produce that which is higher. If soul be superior in kind to matter, then it cannot be a result of matter. If reason and conscience be more in kind than is the body, neither is the body nor are the causes which may account for the body efficient for their production. The primitive inferior cannot produce the primitive superior. Mind having existence in man, and being unaccounted for by matter, makes logically true and acceptable the alternative that the "universe was caused by a self-existent being" or soul.

The soul of man, therefore, is a creation of the Over-Soul. It is linked to that Being by bonds of nature. Are not those bonds indissoluble? Can anything destroy the connection between an animal or human progenitor and its offspring? How strong soever the desire to sever the union, is it possible to accomplish the task? A parent may drive his son from his home, deprive him of the felicities of the household, treat him with scorn and disinherit him. Is the child not always a son to that father? There being no denial in such instances, surely there can be none as regards the human soul and the Soul which has produced it.

As to the *character* of the Creator, men long wondered and studiously meditated. Was he bad or was he good? Thousands of years humanity waited and watched, hoping to determine. But it was not until the " Light of the World " shone forth that men were able to discern clearly. Then they learned, through simple yet profound teaching, that God always has been, and forever will be, good. The disclosure of this fact as a reality, undying and revivifying, was both marvellous and inspiring. It lent not only grandeur to the course of history, but sublimity to the human soul.

A Being who was good — eternally and absolutely good — could produce nothing bad or wrong. Especially would it be contrary to the nature of things for such a Soul to make a soul altogether and in every particular " inclined to all evil." The resultant soul must partake of the characteristics and unique qualities of its Producer. The latter being good, the former must be. At least the former must have decided latent tendency to that which is good and pure. And, inasmuch as the soul is made "in the image" of its Creator, — made a soul having judgment and moral discernment, — we must think of it as possessing potential goodness to a degree sufficient to control and dominate it.

What shall make that goodness active? How shall it overcome the contemporaneous vicious tendencies of human nature? For nobody can deny that these exist. With freedom to choose, can it be that a soul with strong propensities to unholiness will be directed to holiness? Will not such direction destroy the soul's freedom? Can the good be made the dominant quality of the life of the individual and he remain within the circle of his liberty? The reply must always be that, since the soul is a creation and offspring of God, such results must ensue. Else there is an ulcer in the moral universe, and God's goodness meets with ignominious defeat in its transmission and operations.

The apprehension of the method by which souls are transformed may be clearer and more distinct if we investigate some of the things with which we are tolerably familiar.

Imagine that we are at the beginning of spring.

For four long months there has been a chill in the atmosphere, and the leaves have blown about the streets. There have been storms of sleet and snow. Animals have hibernated, and man has partially secluded himself that the winter frosts might not injure him. The invalid, the mother with a babe in her arms, the aged taking their last lingering steps on earth, have found it a period of undesired imprisonment, of increased care, and of decided deprivation. At last the spring-time, with its vigorous throb of energy, has come. On every side are manifestations of renewal. The grass that has lain brown so long is being dotted with green. Blades here and there, growing in size, and increasing in number, wrap, at length, the whole earth in a mantle of beauty. The birds are returning. On the recurring mornings we hear their glad voices. How sweet their songs! The sap in the trees mounts aloft, and from out the branches come the twigs and the leaves. On every bush by the roadside and in the field, we see the buds which prophesy blossoms and fruit. A wonderful transformation has been wrought. How? Ah! that is the secret. Maybe we shall learn as the season progresses.

We watch the development and scrutinize the unfolding, until at length the autumn comes. A beautiful night succeeds a beautiful day. No clouds shut out the light of heaven as its rays sparkle and stream through the myriad windows of the firmament. King Frost sallies forth from the North with his chariot and fiery steeds. Travelling until the dawn of day, he touches the plants and growing vines with his icy fingers. The leaves are seared. The grass is browned. There are drooping heads all about us. Ripened grain and fruit are made ready for the garner. When several nights like this have passed, we climb to some hill-top and cast our eye over the fields and mountain-side. What a view! Did ever one behold such coloring! Beautiful reds and yellows! What a picture! Where can we secure like tints! — are the exclamations. It is wonderful and it is fascinating. No lover of nature can look about him in the autumn-time and not be charmed and inspired. Marvellous, marvellous is the task accomplished. How has it been, wrought? we ask. But still that remains a secret.

Were we to stand beside some great cathedral

during its construction, we should perceive the blocks of stone, the heavy timbers, and all the materials requisite to the completion of the pile. We should also see the men employed, their tools and machinery.

Were we to enter the machine-shop, we might look upon a locomotive. It stands before us, seemingly conscious of its might and power. Looking at it carefully, we detect many dissimilar parts, yet each adapted to a specific purpose. As a whole, it is to draw a train freighted with humanity. We are told its capacity, and the tale is verified by a test. After riding seventy-five or eighty miles an hour, we inquire as to the method of its construction. We are shown men, lathes, wrenches, hammers, and a hundred other things, which in their combined capacity have made the huge machine possible.

Were we to enter a studio and watch the sculptor at his work, we should see his block of marble or granite; we should see his model and its marked measurings; we should see him manipulate his sharpened steel; and we should behold the figure gradually emerge, well-proportioned, from the rough-hewn stone.

In all these things we detect not only results, but, as well, the means and method whereby the results are achieved. If it be desirable, we can calculate the force of muscle and of heat and other elementary energies expended in producing these results. There is very little of anything that is beyond the ken and measurement of the expert and specialist in any of these departments of man's activity.

It is not so in the changes from winter to spring, nor from summer to autumn. We can but note the alterations of all the things round about us. What of the agency producing those changes? Can we see it? Can we touch it? Can we hear it? Can we measure it? Indeed, can we detect it, as it works, by any sense, or by anything similar to sense? If not, to what conclusion must we come? Surely we are justified, alike by observation, experience, history, and philosophy, in asserting that all the transformations wrought in the outer world are wrought by an invisible power. The elements are all within an Unseen Hand, and they are fashioned as a potter fashions the clay. Some power other than that resident within moulds them.

If, then, external and material substances may be affected from without themselves, it would not be strange to conceive of a human soul being affected by powers or influences external to itself.

The soul is a creation, with the possibilities of both evil and good. Every soul is such. In some the former dominates; in others, the latter. In the majority, evil seems to be uppermost. If there could be a spiritual affecting of the soul whereby the good would march forth from the seclusion of potentiality, and become the active and commanding agent in the arena of individual life, the soul would be reborn, renewed, and would, gradually, become holy. Is such an operation possible?

We need to keep constantly in mind that man is an invisible and spiritual being, and that his Creator is likewise an invisible spiritual Being. If, then, the forces and agents which operate so effectually between material substances for their alteration and improvement are unseen, it cannot possibly be expected that the forces and agents which operate between two spiritual beings will be seen. Indeed, there is far more profound reason for the latter to be regarded as invisible than for the former. And not only so. If man and God be spiritual, the agency by which man is to know God, and, indeed, his fellow-men, is — must be — spiritual. Man, therefore, is to be affected by unseen spiritual influences, and by these is to be rearranged or polarized, morally and spiritually.

Is there doubt as to the existence of such agencies? It seems hardly possible for scepticism in this regard. Make inquiry of a friend as to which had the greater effect upon him, the precepts and instruction of his mother, or her quiet, gentle, trustful, serene, and loving life. If a boy could have lived twenty years in the presence of George Washington, would it not have produced a result in the quality of his character, even though Washington had never given him moral instruction? On the other hand, would not the mere companionship of Nero, Louis XIV., or Henry VIII. have corrupted the boy and made him licentious and dissolute? A father may tell his son not to use tobacco nor to be profane; but if he is himself addicted to both, what of his boy? Do not our associates affect us for evil or for good? I do not seek to undervalue teach-

ing. I only desire the recognition of another and
more subtile agency at work in the world.

What is that agency? It has never been seen,
never been touched, never been weighed. To the
performance of its task there has been no apparent
gathering of forces. Every stage of the procedure has been noiseless and without appearance.
Man's influence over man is the influence of an
invisible soul over an invisible soul, — an influence in itself as invisible as its source and its
recipient. It is a spiritual influence.

But the human, as already indicated, has unique
relationships to the Divine, the created to the
Creator. Shall it be asserted that the realm of
spiritual influence is limited to that of the lower
world and human intercourse? If one man may
influence the soul of another man, may we not
believe that there are also soul or spiritual influences of a higher grade?

It is most reasonable to believe in an immanent
God. The Divine is not only above the world
and distinct from the world, but he is in the
world. Law has not been ordained and left to
self-execution. God is operating. The universe
is not a vast machine once set in motion by the

Unseen, who, having started it, then retired. It is the Unseen which supplies the motive power, and forces the constant movement.

If, then, God be in the world, man must be subject to the influence of that Presence. If the shrubs and rocks, the sea and the sky, respond to His demands and commands, much more must man. As a spiritual being he ought, in the nature of the case, to be more sensitive to the presence of the Father-Spirit than is any non-spiritual substance. To deny that such sensitiveness is possible would be to assert that spirit is utterly unresponsive to spirit. Such an assertion is proven absolutely untrue. If we observe the transformation of character all about us, if we believe in what men tell us, and if we accept the verdict of our own experience, we must conclude that the spirit of God affects the spirit of man to the enlargement, unfolding, edification, and redemption of the latter.

Here is the very heart-centre of human existence. Man, as the kin of God, is to be influenced, upbuilded, and moulded by him. "No man hath seen God at any time" is as true to-day as ever. But that is not saying that no man

hath FELT God at any time. To affirm the
latter would be a falsehood. Jesus said, " This
is eternal life, that men might know thee the
only true God, and Jesus Christ whom thou hast
sent." If men are to have that life, then there
must be some sort of knowledge of God.

To what sort of knowledge is it probable Jesus
referred? If a man studies the firmament with
the telescope, or the insect-world with the micro-
scope, or studies any other physical phenomena,
will he know God? He may, and he may not.
Natural scientists disagree in their conclusions as
to the existence of a Creator. Does anybody
claim that Jesus was a " scientist" or a man
" learned in the schools"? And will not all
claim that he, of all who ever walked the earth,
had in him the " eternal life"? If so, he must
have known God. That makes it evident that
one devoid of technical education, one who is
" unlettered and unlearned," may " know God,"
and thereby have " life."

But how? By becoming conscious of the presence of the Invisible. If some metaphysicians
deny that such consciousness is possible, let no
one be dismayed. There are scores upon scores

of individuals who will persistently assert that they know God directly and immediately, without an intervening agency. They will assert that they feel God within themselves when they place themselves in proper spiritual attitude. And we may judge from the course of many lives — some transformed from extreme sinfulness, and others saved from the more ordinary erring of men — that what is so confidently asserted is true. For many such there are who live the Christ-like, or the " eternal " life.

Man, therefore, may be moulded by this Invisible Being. While it is true that we are affected more or less by influences of which we are not conscious, it is likewise true that we are affected most truly by influences of which we are conscious. There are certain conditions under which the Invisible may work his most complete work in us. To intentionally close the way of access to the soul, and to persistently keep it closed, will make growth in divineness of character exceedingly slow, if indeed not utterly impossible. Simply to be passive, and allow the sunlight of heaven to shine upon the soul, will produce some growth, inevitably; though it will be disheartening and discouraging.

But to be open-souled and eager for assistance to holiness, to be desirous of employing every instrumentality which will promote purity and godliness, that is the condition through which heavenliness of life increases with greatest rapidity, and in which moral strength and spiritual beauty become most pronounced, invincible, and sublime.

Phillips Brooks says : —

" Let the frost smite your cheek, let the rain beat into your face, let the wind blow upon your back, and then you know by personal experience what you had known by your observation before. I say that only when a man puts himself where he can feel the power of the Christ, where it is possible for him, if there be a Christ, if Christ be all that the Christian religion claims that he is, only when a man puts himself where he needs and must have and must certainly feel that Christ, if there be a Christ, only then has he a right to disbelieve if the Christ be not there, only then has he a right to believe if the Christ find him there."

To be moulded by the Invisible is the opportunity of opportunities. In a world so full of marvels and mystery, with a nature so charged with potentiality, it is our privilege to become righteous and holy. What a privilege that is ! It means that we are to have our thought so clarified

as to perceive basal truths, and as to fail not to
permit them to lead us to their legitimate results.
It means that our choices and our conduct will be
compatible with our conceptions.   It means that
revenge, impulse, passion, and all else of the
lower and unworthy, will be subjected to that
which is highest and best.   Indeed, to be moulded
by the Invisible signifies that we shall be growing
away from all that is evil, and that love (the free,
voluntary outreaching of our spirits) will become
the motive in all our considerations, the manifest
force in all our intercourse, and the quickener of
all our aspirations.

THE UPLIFT OF PRAYER.

CHARLES ROCKWELL TENNEY.

THE UPLIFT OF PRAYER.

PRAYER is desire consciously depending upon God's help for realization of its object. Observe, it is desire depending upon God. The sense of God, and belief that he is, or may be, propitious, are essential, are fundamental. So, properly speaking, and however God may meet it, mere desire is not prayer. Need is not prayer, and it is only by a figure of speech that we can say that the tree or the flower prays. They have their needs, and would die if God did not fill the cups which are held up toward heaven on their account; but they are neither conscious of the need, nor of the only source of supply, therefore they do not pray. So far as we know, or can know, only man prays; and he only as the sense of need hath over against it the sense of a Power which can, and, if the conditions can be made right, which will, serve the need. Already Montgomery's hymn has been suggested, and the reader has said to himself:

"Prayer is the soul's sincere desire,
    Uttered or unexpressed."

And that were good if we did not stop there. It is true that prayer is prayer, whether " uttered or unexpressed ; " but it is entirely false to use these two lines, as they so often are used, as an answer to the question, What is prayer? The author would not have had them used in this way. Desire, however sincere, is not prayer ; and we must read at least two stanzas of the hymn to find out what prayer is. Then we find out that the poet's idea was that " the sincere desire," " the burden of a sigh," " the falling of a tear," " the upward glancing of an eye," become prayer only as the sense of God is present, only as they come of conscious dependence upon his help, only

"When none but God is near."

To wish or to desire is not to pray. To desire of God is to pray.

But what is the uplift of prayer? Is it when one uplifts himself in prayer? or is it when he is uplifted in answer to his prayer? Why not both? Is it not the first as the necessary condition of the

second? Is it not the second as the only adequate result and justification of the first? It is
like this: When we have done the best we could,
and our desire is still unsatisfied, our own high
instincts encourage, in great stress constrain, us
to pray. We turn the pages of the world's history, and we find the holiest in all ages praying.
We open the pages of inspiration, and, in no
uncertain terms, find ourselves bidden to pray.
Now, since from its very nature prayer cannot
be merely for the sake of praying, do not these
voices utter the one promise, "Ask, and ye shall
receive"? Do they not emphasize the one great
assurance that God will heed our call, and come
to our need? Do they not distinctly commend
prayer, not as a crutch for our incompetency, but
as the lever for our strength — the lever with
which we may lift from our path the largest difficulties, and pry open the great doors of the
kingdom? Manifestly great things are conditioned upon prayer, and he doeth well who prays.
The uplift of prayer, then, shall, *must*, mean
first the voluntary uplift upon which the extra
or super-voluntary depends.

But then it must mean also this extra-voluntary

uplift, for it is this which the voluntary hath contemplated, and in which it finds its justification. Some say, " Pray, for so you will come to a better understanding of your needs; " or, " Pray, for prayer is a good spiritual exercise, and will generate spiritual warmth and magnetism." Now, it is doubtless true that real prayer helps by indirection and reaction; but prayer that is made merely for the incidental results is not real, and must be so conscious of the insincerity involved that it cannot long persist. He who bids us pray merely that we may help ourselves is trifling with us. The only justification of prayer to God is that God hears and answers it; and this, God's answer, is the ultimate and divine uplift which comes of prayer, and which our subject contemplates.

We proceed, then, to think upon the uplift of prayer, giving our attention, first, to the voluntary uplift, or the uplift involved in the act of praying; and, second, to the extra-voluntary uplift, or the uplift which comes as the answer to prayer.

And first the voluntary uplift. This, or the beginning of it, is when we determine to pray.

And at the beginning the uplift may be from a very low level; for we are not praying from the heights, but towards them; not at the finish, but at the start. There will be a prayer appropriate for the finish and the heights, a prayer breaking into praise and thanksgiving; but the uplift of prayer does not *begin* there. Indeed, it begins when we are farthest from all that, when we are most oppressed by sense of sinfulness, littleness, need. Then, when the sense of God, never quite absent from any soul, presses itself upon us as our only hope; then, when some voice, within or without, says, " Ask, and ye shall receive; " then, when we first say, I *will* " ask of God, who giveth to all men liberally and upbraideth not," — then is the beginning of prayer and the uplift of prayer. " But," some one will say, " the initiative is not in the will, for ' it is God who worketh in you both to will and to do of his good pleasure.' " True; but, after all, practically, the initiative is with you, for the working of God within availeth not until you engage yourself to " work out your own salvation with anxiety and self-distrust." " The intercession of the Spirit " is prevented until you are ready to say, " God help me."

And it is good to see that the first thing is the
will to pray, for many think they must wait until
they "feel like it." And by this they do not
mean that they must wait for a sense of need and
an impulse to go to God with that need; but
they think that prayer cometh properly only out
of some rapture, some ecstasy of the soul. But
now we have learned that we are not to wait to
"feel like it," but are resolutely, earnestly, to do
it. If the rapture comes afterwards and incidentally, well and good; but the initial and essential
thing is the will to pray. Some one exclaims,
"What, pray when your hearts are cold?" And
some one else aptly replies, "Yes, by all means;
suppose your hands are cold, do you wait for
them to become warm before going to the fire?"
It is not the experience and then the prayer, but
the prayer that we may have the experience. So
the purpose is the beginning of the uplift.

But after one hath purposed to pray, he prayeth, and this raiseth him higher. He hath lifted
his eyes unto the hills, now he climbeth them.
He hath said, I will seek my Father, and now he
seeketh him. Is it not an uplift when a man
wrests his attention from the darkness, and per-

sistently fixes it upon the light; when he ceases looking into the muddy pools of earth, perhaps seeing nothing better than his own reflection in them, and looks upon the pure heavens, and upon him who is enthroned over all? Is it not an uplift when, even for a little, a man ceases to talk with those who are beneath, that he may talk with him who is above? Verily his "conversation is in heaven," and "conversation" in heaven is sure ultimately to be translated into "citizenship" in heaven. For as one perseveres in prayer, the will to pray grows stronger, and the way to pray grows clearer; the hold upon him of the forces which would keep him down becomes weaker, and the face of the Eternal, vaguely sought and seen at the beginning, becomes more distinct. Yes, these results follow if one perseveres in prayer. He may get none of the specific things for which he asks; but he certainly will get a better acquaintance with him before whom he hath appeared, and a better understanding of his will. And there can be no doubt but his own desires will be greatly qualified, as he holds them up in the light, and tells them over to the pure One. There can be no doubt but one who prays

learns to desire fewer and better things. Indeed,
as in this light he contemplates the foolishness
of much that he hath wished, and the wisdom of
him to whom he hath come, it is almost sure that
he will rise more and more toward the spiritual
height of him who subjected his own desires, and
said, under the stress and agony of the strongest
of them, only this : " If it be possible . . . nevertheless not my will, but thine, be done." And all
this uplift of purpose, of mind, of heart, of habit,
you see is not of the answer to prayer, but of the
praying.

And the uplift involved in praying is surer because he who perseveres will avail himself of all
favorable conditions and all helps to it. Generally speaking, it is only he in whom, consciously
or unconsciously, scorn of the fact is growing, who
scorns the forms of prayer. The genuinely prayerful will by no means cease praying because there
is no prescribed form which serveth the occasion,
or because some customary attitude is inconven-
ient. If he has not learned a prayer which fitteth
the need, he will make one ; and if it is not con-
venient to stand or kneel, he will pray sitting or
walking or driving ; and if he may not bow his

head and close his eyes, yet will he pray. But let him question if his prayerfulness is not waning who never feels an impulse to shut his eyes upon every earthly thing, and bow down, nay, prostrate himself, before the Majesty on high. But the point is, he who really prays will help himself by every suggestive form and attitude ; and if his lips do not teach his knees, his knees will remind his lips, to pray. And he will help himself by seeking such companionships as are helpful, remembering the great promise which hinges upon the consent of any two as to what they shall ask, or which is given to two or three gathered together in the name of the Good. And while he prayeth much in company, that the faith and fervor of others may help his own, he will prize much more the privilege of solitude, and, with Jesus, will frequently go apart to pray, where being still will help him to know God, and where nothing shall disturb the glad outpouring of his heart. And while every place, and all the ways in which he walks, and all occasions, are hallowed with the prayers he breathes, it is not because he is indifferent to special places and appointed times. The man of prayer is ever saying, —

> " How amiable are thy tabernacles,
>   O Lord of hosts !
>   My soul longeth, yea, even fainteth
>   for the courts of the Lord !"

and ever singing, —

> "Sweet hour of prayer ! sweet hour of prayer !"

The place and the time are not unimportant to him. He helpeth the uplift of his soul by all that can be found in hallowed associations and habits of devotion.

And yet otherwise does praying lift him. Persisted in, it shames him out of conduct that is incongruous, and stimulates him to that which is harmonious, consistent. Real prayer will not compound with impurity, falsehood, hate, idleness, cowardice, self-indulgence, pride, or any such thing. It is as intolerant of all these as water is of oil. If a man will persist in prayer, will keep its pure flood flowing from his life, it will float all these evils out, and cast them up to be consumed. But if, on the other hand, he will persist in these, or any of them, they will effectually dam the current Godward of all aspiration and desire, and he will have to say with the wicked king : —

> " Pray can I not,
> Though inclination be as sharp as will ;
> My stronger guilt defeats my strong intent;
> And like a man to double business bound,
> I stand in pause where I shall first begin,
> And both neglect."

There are those who " for a pretence make long prayers." Their prayers are not prayers, but pretences. All sorts of wickedness are consistent with such hypocrisy But real prayer, the voluntary uplift of the soul into the presence of the Pure, demands of the soul that it become pure.

And it requires not only that the soul rid itself of impurity, but that it engage itself in all good offices and faithful work. As illustrating, perhaps covering, the various positive virtues, real prayer commits one to industry and charity. It commits him to industry; and the challenge of the apostle is always in order, " Show me thy faith without thy works, and I will show thee my faith by my works." Unless there is nothing else that he can do, he who lies upon his back and longs for things, even though he holds up his idle hands towards God for them, has not yet learned how to pray. Real prayer does not say to enterprise,

Take in your sails; wrap yourself in your hammock; your toils are past. It says rather, Call all hands upon deck; to the last shred spread forth your sails; do your utmost; trust God for the rest. Real prayer is not an extinguisher upon zeal, but a breath fanning it to brighter use. Indeed, the truer rendering of St. James v. 16 shows it a form of industry. It is " in its working " that it avails. And its working is not always in words. It works in deeds as well, and, with the reverent man, planting and digging and casting his nets are but forms of praying. For see, there is no force in the planting to make the harvest, or in the digging to produce the gold, or in the casting of the nets to create the fish. It is God who " giveth the increase." The prayerful man knoweth this; and his labors become prayers, and he does not forget to thank God for the results. Bayard Taylor says, " Labor, you know, is prayer." Yes, if it be reverent labor, labor depending upon God. But he who works, cursing the necessity that he must work, is not praying. Emerson says, " The prayer of the farmer kneeling in his field to weed it, the prayer of the rower kneeling with the stroke of his oar, are

true prayers." They are *if* they are, not otherwise. If they are an expression of desire consciously depending upon God for the realization of
its object, then are they prayers. But how is it
when the spirit of the farmer and rower are full
of blasphemy, and when they are thinking of no
good thing toward God or any one? All prayer
works, but, alas, all work does not pray. But the
point is, prayer raises the soul to higher levels
because it commits to consistent endeavors. And,
looking back through the centuries, you will find
that this is so — that those who have prayed best
have worked best, and that the great endeavors
which have transformed the world have had beginning in the garden, on the mountain, in the
prayer-house, in the closet, where men have received their patterns and inspirations from Him
who " worketh hitherto " and evermore.

But this is more evidently true because true
prayer binds to charity as well as industry. It is
impossible that one should come into such conscious dependence upon the love of God as is
implied by the fact that he prays without at once
coming into a state of mind, gentle, favorable,
propitious, toward any who may in any way be

served by him. He may come to the altar with his offering and his petition, but then will he be moved to leave his gift before the altar that he may ask pardon, and make reparation to his brother whom he hath wronged; after that, he will come and offer his gift. If it be real, prayer exacts submission to, compliance with, imitation of, that Love which it supplicates.

> " We do pray for mercy,
> And that same prayer doth teach us all to render
> The deeds of mercy."

Prayer not only works, but loves. This is the meaning, no doubt, of Coleridge's couplet, —

> " He prayeth best who loveth best,
> All things, both great and small."

And this may be a test of our prayers; for if they do not result in making us more loving, we have not yet learned how to pray.

And this is a part — does it not appear so? — of the voluntary uplift of prayer, a part of the uplift involved in the act of praying. So much hath he who hath willed to pray done for himself. By use of prayer he hath kindled desire for every form of good. It was his to take the initiative; and this that we have seen, and more for which this stands, was involved in it. The uplift of prayer is first a voluntary uplift.

First, but not chiefly. The voluntary is in order to the extra- or super-voluntary; the praying is for the sake of the answer to prayer; and when one hath thus uplifted himself he expects God will uplift him, bearing him to heights which, unaided, he cannot hope to reach. And it is the very essence of religion, of Christianity, at least, to affirm that God will do this very thing, that he hears and answers prayer; indeed, that he reserves some of his best gifts, perhaps some of the best of every gift, until our need and our sense of dependence upon him become distinct and urgent enough to lead us humbly and earnestly to ask him for them. Then he gives the gift, and better gifts. And this is the uplift of prayer.

And, in this second part, it begins when God takes the prayer, and sets it among the reasons upon which his action is to depend. The man pursued by urgent need and by the sense of God cannot help praying; how does his soul take courage when he knows that God, filled with the love of his child, can no more help hearing. Your request is heard and recorded in heaven, and hath weight there. The specific thing may or may not be granted, but it will be more likely to be granted because you have prayed. As Dr. Clarke has said: "Just as, when a man ploughs the ground and plants his seed, he co-operates with divine laws, the natural result of which is a harvest; so, when a man prays for anything he really wants, and while he prays endeavors to abide in the spirit of Christ and pray out of that, he co-operates with other divine laws, the natural result of which is the receiving what he asks. Not always, not always in either case. The man may plough and sow, and no crop come; still there is a tendency in ploughing and sowing to make the crop come. A man may pray for his sick child's recovery, and the child die nevertheless. But there *was a tendency in his prayer* to save his child's life." So your prayer is heard in heaven. God hath received it. In this are not both it and you lifted up? And, unless the objections are insuperable, so that to answer with the thing you ask would not be to bestow the blessing you desire, God answers your prayer —

is not this to be exalted? In the fact that God attends and answers is there uplift in prayer.

How must Abraham have rejoiced in it when he knew himself recognized of God as he prayed before him! So high does he appear in view of all this that we call him the "Friend of God." And Ishmael is but a little boy, and more despised because he is the son of the handmaid; yet can he cry so as to be heard on high; and the messenger saith to Hagar, his mother, "Fear not, for God hath heard the voice of the lad where he is." And Jacob wrestles in prayer, and proves what force is in it, inasmuch as the answer is given only to his perseverance; and he is named Israel because, as a prince, hath he power with God and with men, and hath prevailed. And to Joseph in Egypt were secrets shown when he prayed, and to Daniel in Babylon, and to David and the prophets. And in the New Testament how strongly hath God bound himself to heed the requests of his children! In the promises he hath opened a way for the poorest of us to stand beside him, that we may tell him our reasons, and make known our requests. How is the promise iterated and emphasized: "Ask, and it shall be given you; seek, and ye shall find; knock, and it shall be opened unto you: for everyone that asketh receiveth; and he that seeketh findeth; and to him who knocketh it shall be opened." "And all things whatsoever ye shall ask in prayer, believing, ye shall receive." "And whatsoever ye shall ask in my name, that will I do, that the Father may be glorified in the Son." "If ye abide in me, and my words abide in you, ask whatsoever ye will, and it shall be done unto you." "Verily, verily, I say unto you, if ye shall ask anything of the Father, he will give it you in my name. Hitherto ye have asked nothing in my name: ask and ye shall receive, that your joy may be fulfilled." And these promises are multiplied, and the exhortations to prayerfulness are upon almost every page of the New Testament. And, as of old the force which is in prayer had been revealed to Jacob's persistency, so in the teachings of Jesus is it revealed when, in the parables of the friend at midnight, and the importunate widow, he shows that "men ought always to pray and not to faint;" the reason and encouragement being that, if prayer hath force to constrain unwillingness, it must be of far greater force with him whose willingness hath ordained it, and only waits that it be made with due earnestness and faith.

But its force is even more impressively taught by the conduct of Jesus. His office was to show us what God is like, and what is his disposition toward his children. And how accessible he was! Was any need which came to him unanswered? This means that no need shall be brought to God which shall not in some way, in the best way, be answered. A leper hails him and says, "Thou canst make me clean." He doth not withdraw from, but compassionately touches him, answering his prayer. The paralytic is brought, and the divine discourse is interrupted as his friends illustrate the truth that real prayer works as well as prays. Jesus is not offended, but bids the paralytic go home, bearing his bed. A woman in the throng would secretly avail herself of the health which is in him. This, however, she could not do; nevertheless, because her touch was genuine, the gift she sought was given. A man prayeth for his son, another for his servant, another for his daughter. These prayers for *others* are allowed, and the son and

servant, though far away, are cured; and the little daughter, dead when he cometh to the place,
is raised to life again. And then, as now, there
were those who thought that prayer was (at least
sometimes) an impertinence. When the Ca-
naanite woman importuned for the deliverance of
her daughter from an unclean spirit, and when
the blind men, at the gates of Jericho, clamored
for the restoration of their sight, these would have
silenced and sent them away. But he was not
offended by their earnestness; he gave himself
to their need. And he doth not wait that men
be worthy to be answered. Did he, how hopeless
it were to pray! Ten lepers come, and, though
only one hath grace enough to return him thanks,
all are cleansed. So doth it appear that, apart
from everything beside, even apart from virtue,
prayer hath force, a force its own. And by these
examples does Jesus impress the conviction that
God, whom he represents, is not far off, inacces-
sible, but present, ready to hear, easy to be en-
treated. So does he show us, by his acts, how
God honors prayer by making his omnipotence
to flow through the gates it opens. The real
uplift of prayer is in this, that God answers it,

that " Good prayers never come weeping home."
And what an uplift this is ! In the darkness one
has been reaching up and feeling after God;
what joy to find the divine hand reaching down
for him ! He holds upon that hand, grasping it
firmly lest he lose it; what joy to feel its answering pressure, as if it would not be lost !

And this answer to prayer men have known,
not in the Bible times alone, but in all the years.
The testimony of Sir Fowell Buxton, quoted by
Professor Phelps, could be repeated by multitudes. He says, " When I am out of heart I
follow David's example, and fly for refuge to
prayer. . . . I am bound to acknowledge that
I have always found that my prayers have been
heard and answered. . . . I understand literally
the injunction : ' In everything make your requests known to God ; ' and I cannot but notice
how amply these prayers have been met." Again,
he writes to his daughter concerning a division
in the House of Commons in the conflict for
West Indian emancipation: " What led to that
division ? If ever there was a subject which occupied our prayers, it was this. Do you remember how we desired that God would give me his

spirit in that emergency; how we quoted the
promise, ‘He that lacketh wisdom, let him ask
it of the Lord, and it *shall* be given him;’ and
how I kept open that passage in the Old Testament, in which it is said, ‘We have no might
against this great company that cometh against
us, neither know we what to do, but our eyes
are upon thee’ — the Spirit of the Lord reply-
ing, ‘Be not afraid nor dismayed by reason of
this great multitude, for the battle is not yours,
but God's’? If you want to see the passage, open
my Bible; it will turn of itself to the place. I
sincerely believe that *prayer* was the cause of
that division; and I am confirmed in this by
knowing that we by no means calculated on the
effect.” Testimonies, instances, like this, could
be multiplied indefinitely. They mean that to-
day God hears and answers prayer — that Jesus
made visible the attention with which God always honors it. If it is possible, he answers it
in kind; but, if the prayer is real, he always
answers in some kind. Says an old English divine, “I am sure I shall receive either what I
ask or what I should ask.” But the point is,
God hears thee, and thy prayer hath a *tendency*

to bring the specific thing it seeks. And this is the uplift of prayer.

But not this alone. God gives the gift, and better gifts. He pours his omnipotence through the gates which prayer opens, but not merely upon the wheels which prayer hath set for it. The flood of good is sure to overflow all bounds, and variously bless the life. And here the two parts of our discourse overlap each other and become confused. We have said that the voluntary uplift, the act of praying, strengthens the will and makes clearer the way to pray, that, as one perseveres, desire is purified, the hold of the forces that keep down becomes weaker, and the soul is more and more committed to all that is good. And this must be true. These are natural results. But when one truly prays are they wholly left to nature? Not for a moment. Indeed, the answer anticipates, crowds upon, the asking, inasmuch as "it is God who worketh within you both to will and to do of his good pleasure," inasmuch as it is God, who, unrecognized, prompts all pure desire. And the desire becomes purified as it is lifted up to the pure One, does it? That surely is natural and reasonable. But not so alone is it purified; for, while thou prayest, God pours his desire for thee into thy bosom that it may become thine; and so the Spirit maketh intercession for thee. This it is which brings thee surely to that spiritual uplift of the Master, toward which thine own volition to pray tendeth, in which he said, "Not my will, but thine, be done." And, as thou prayest, the will to pray grows stronger, does it? Yes, naturally, as when one exercises any power it grows stronger by the exercise. But is there not an experience to the devout beyond this? Early hath he not felt another Will beneath his own, and lifting him to heights he could not hope to reach alone?

> "A mighty wind of nobler will
>   Sends through his soul its quickening thrill;
>   No more a creature of the clod,
>   He knows himself a child of God."

And is conscience quickened? As we have seen, so must it be with one who prays. But not alone because he prays; more because God answers him. He, with clear vision, sees and hates the evil things that crawl and hide within; but it is so because the flood of grace, sweeping to the point to which his prayers have bidden it, has washed his vision clear that he may see; or it is so because the light, invoked for special use, has lighted all the corners and closets of his room. And is ambition stirred so thou wouldst work as well as pray, proving thy piety by thine industry? It is God giving himself to the regeneration of his world, and the building of his kingdom through thee. And doth thy spirit grow in love toward everything? In thy sphere dost thou feel thyself bound to imitate his mercy? Ah, it is not merely because thou seest how good he is, but because when thou openest the door in prayer his love comes into thy heart, to be, if thou wilt not crush it, the life and love of your love evermore. So doth God give, not sparingly, carefully fitting his answers to our petitions, but "abundantly, above all that we ask or think."

Nor is this all. The uplift of prayer finally bringeth one to transcendent vision and experience. We recall Moses, when he came to the back of the desert, to the mountain of God, even to Horeb. We remember how the vision he sought transcended his expectation, how he was overwhelmed by the revelation of the Eternal, so

that he hid his face, being afraid to look on God.
We remember how God disclosed his presence and
power when Elijah prayed, and the place was
wrapped about with fire, which consumed "the
burnt sacrifice, and the wood, and the stones, and
the dust," and licked up the water that was in
the trenches about the altar; "and all the people saw it, and fell on their faces, and said, The
Lord he is God, the Lord he is God." We remember Paul, the man of prayer, and what transcendent vision came to him when he was lifted
up "to the third heaven," when he was "caught
up into paradise, and heard unspeakable words,
which it is not lawful for a man to utter." We
remember St. John, a prisoner upon the island of
Patmos. We remember the sea beating mono-
tonously about him, making visible and audible
his loneliness. We remember him "in the Spirit
on the Lord's day," and how, in the exaltation of
that hour, there was to him "no more sea." We
remember that the throne-room of the universe
was open to his vision, and that he was lifted to
the presence of him that sitteth upon the throne,
and to the presence of the Lamb. And the vision
opened upon the future, and upon "a new heaven

and a new earth," when " the tabernacle of God shall be with men," when he shall " wipe away all tears from their eyes," and " there shall be no more death, neither sorrow nor crying, neither shall there be any more pain; for the former things are passed away." We remember Jesus and his transfiguration, and that it was "as he prayed" that " the fashion of his countenance was altered, and his raiment was white and glistering." We recall that it was then that Moses and Elijah appeared in a glory which smote awake the heavy eyes of the apostles, and made them long permanently to abide in the divine altitude and experience to which they had been raised when the Master prayed. We recall the cloud, Jehovah's token, which overshadowed, filling them with fear, and the voice from the cloud commending the "beloved Son." And then the voice was past, the cloud gone. Jesus touched them and said, " Arise, be not afraid." They rose to take up again the tasks of every day, and to go forward with a better trust in him whom they had seen when his prayer was answered in the glory of the transfiguration.

But some one is ready to say, These experiences

are reserved for prophets, saints, and Saviours; we may not hope for them. Nay, but common men have enjoyed such approaches to them as to make them seem altogether possible to any who may but learn to pray; and in the life-stories of many whose times touch on ours, is it discovered that true prayer is not infrequently blessed with uplifts similar. It has been written of Edward Payson, a New England divine, "that his mind at times almost lost its sense of the external world, in the ineffable thoughts of God's glory, which rolled like a sea of light around him, at the throne of grace." Of Cowper also, "that, in one of the few lucid hours of his religious life, such was the experience of God's presence which he enjoyed in prayer, that, as he tells us, he thought he should have died with joy, if special strength had not been imparted to bear the disclosure." And the same author tells of one of the Tennents, "that, on one occasion, when he was engaged in secret devotion, so overpowering was the revelation of God which opened upon his soul, and with augmenting intensity of effulgence as he prayed, that at length he recoiled from the intolerable joy as from a pain, and besought God to withhold from him further manifestations of his glory. He said, 'Shall thy servant *see* thee and live?'" And our author continues, "We read of the 'sweet hours' which Edwards enjoyed on the banks of Hudson River, in secret converse with God, and hear his own description of the inward sense of Christ, which at times came into his heart, and which he 'knows not how to express otherwise than by a calm, sweet abstraction of soul from all the concerns of this world; and sometimes a kind of vision . . . of being alone in the mountains, or some solitary wilderness, far from all mankind, sweetly conversing with Christ, and rapt and swallowed up in God.'"

Is it still urged that these experiences are rare? Not so rare. It was out of experience *like* this that, in her poor home and in her last sickness, the only leisure that her life had known perhaps, an untaught woman, who had been used all her life to the roughest kind of work, said to her minister, as he stood beside her to pray, "Those folks are richest who beg most." She had learned how to make the "durable riches" her own. No, these experiences, or approaches to them, are not rare; or, if they are, the fault is not on his part, but on ours. By whatever may serve it, let us make the voluntary uplift, and the super-voluntary shall be the thing we ask, better things, the vision and experience of God himself. From whatever depths, let us faithfully pray toward the heights, and God will lift us to them. The uplift of prayer begins with thee ; God finishes it.

THE OBLIGATIONS OF RELIGION.

Joseph Kimball Mason.

THE OBLIGATIONS OF RELIGION.

RELIGION is an everlasting reality. The latest utterances of science, philosophy, and poetry confirm our faith in its permanence and power.

" We have at length reached a point," says Dr. John Fiske, " where it is becoming daily more and more apparent that, with deeper study of nature, the old strife between faith and knowledge is drawing to a close; and, thus disentangled at last from the ancient slough of despond, the human mind will breathe a freer air, and enjoy a vastly extended horizon."

The late Ernest Renan finds in Christ's teachings, " the sure word on which the edifice of eternal religion shall rest, the pure worship of no date which all lofty souls will practise to the end of time ; and, having run through the whole circle of errors, mankind will return to them as the imperishable expression of its faith and hope."

Whittier voices the same profound sentiment in these words, —

"The letter fails and systems fall,
　　And every symbol wanes ;
The spirit overbrooding all,
　　Eternal love remains."

So all the thought of the world seems to confirm the reasonable conclusion that religion is as lasting as man himself.

Theology, that is, man's thought about religion, is indeed a progressive science, like chemistry, or the art of government, or the questions of philanthropy and enlightened charity. It is influenced by environment, ruling ideas, and intellectual attainment.

In days of superstition and ignorance, magic and ceremony are identified with religion. In times of cruelty, barbarism, and oppression, the teaching concerning the divine nature and human destiny is colored by the prevailing conceptions of humanity and of justice; while in ages of enlightenment, when general knowledge, scientific thought, and free government prevail, theology becomes reasonable and true to life. So our Christianity may be compared to a stream having its source far up in the mountain snows, but becoming corrupted by the soil through which it passes, as it flows down the hillside; until, emerging finally in pleasant fields, it journeys on for miles over its rocky bed under the light of the sun, becoming pure once more as it moves toward the sea.

The leading thoughts of the present-day theology are the Fatherhood of God, the value of man, the leadership of Christ, — who, in his perfect humanity, is at once the mark toward which we press and the revelation of the divine character, — the regeneration of human society through the acceptance of Christian ideals of conduct, the immortality of the human soul, and the spiritual progress of the race, involving the final and universal triumph of good over evil and so hope eternal for the soul of man. Who will deny that such teaching as this is in accordance with the spirit of the New Testament and is identical with religion itself? We are beginning to know the full meaning of Christ's words, " My joy I give unto you," and to see that this, and not despair, is the secret of the universe. Moreover, though materialism and unbelief prevail far too generally, and the kingdom of heaven is still in the distance, it is our profound conviction that the world was never more truly religious, never nearer to Christ, than it is to-day.

At this point we touch a danger — the danger always attending prosperity — of ignoring the fact that divine blessings are conditioned upon human activity. Every advance that has been made implies human faithfulness and devotion. Nothing comes by chance. We rejoice in what we call the fruits of our Christian civilization, because brave men have lived and toiled in the past, rebuking error and sin in their day, and, one by one, winning the triumphs of light over darkness. So it has been in our progress toward a true theology. We stand on the sunlit heights of vision, but prophets and apostles in every generation have led us there. Hence, to rest upon our religion, and to say, practically, the world will be saved by waiting, and we have nothing to do, is not only our danger, but is contrary to all experience. The very nature of our faith calls us to act in the present moment, and to find in our great hopes no excuse for negligence nor for idleness, but rather an inspiration to join the cloud of witnesses, and share with them the privilege of being co-laborers with God.

Every gift of Heaven to man implies corresponding obligations. Bodily health involves physical activity; mental powers indicate the earnest seeking after knowledge; the possession of wealth lays upon the holder the duty of using the gift for the welfare of the greatest number possible. Positions of honor are bestowed upon men not that they may have personal ease, but that they may render devoted service. Genius implies expression; he who paints or carves or sings must use his gift for the happiness and welfare of his brother, or the gift perishes, and the possessor is dishonored. It is not strange therefore that this principle holds good in religion.

The story is told of one who had always lived far inland, and who stood one summer day upon the shore of the ocean. "Is this all?" he said; "it looks like a tranquil lake." "Yes, this is all." But let this observer wait, and see how much is involved in this seeming calm. Let him observe the tides, as twice a day the great body of waters rolls down into the trough of the sea, or, wonderful and mysterious, flows back again, covering the black wastes, and filling every inlet of the land with the inflowing tide. Or let him, borne forth upon the bosom of this sea, now so quiet, behold the storm arise, feel its mighty power as it tosses the huge vessels like egg-shells on its surface. Let him realize the vastness of this channel of the world's traffic, and he will apprehend more clearly the powers of the sea. It is so with religion. We must know by experience before we appreciate the comprehensiveness of that which, when all things else prove but a rope of sand, uplifts and sustains the soul. It brings peace to the mind indeed, and comfort to the heart, and, more than this, it involves gracious duties and noble obligations. "If ye know these things," said Christ, "happy are ye if ye do them." Religion is not only a reality to be trusted, but a duty to be performed. He who trusts in the Infinite must also heed Christ's injunction, "Thou shalt love the Lord thy God with all thy heart, and with all thy soul, and with all thy mind." Faith in God as an intellectual act most men can understand; but they are not so ready to accept a corresponding obligation of "love of God." The mind seeks to know the cause of things. Not to know the reason of being is to live "where musicians are always

tuning their instruments, but never play a tune."
Hence, most men assume the divine philosophy
in preference to the unsatisfying assumptions of
materialism, and say, with the author of Genesis,
" In the beginning God made the heavens and
the earth."

The problems of physical and moral evil find
no solution so adequate as the assumption of a
loving and all-powerful Being, who will overcome
evil with good. But when we go on, and affirm
that the logical outcome of such faith is to love
the Lord our God, the result is not so generally
realized or accepted. Men say, " How can we
love a being whom we have not seen? Why is it
not sufficient to believe, and rest there?"

In order to answer these questions we must
proceed to definitions. What is the nature of
love? Surely he who spake "as never man
spake" would not imply an obligation that was
an impossibility; moreover, the student of the
gospel is impressed with the fact that every commandment there made is written also in the
nature of things, and may as truly be called
privilege as commandment. " Christianity," says
Dr. Andrew Peabody, "cannot enable us to do

more than the right, nor can the rejection of
Christianity make less than the right incumbent
upon us; but this burden Christ makes light
and easy in two ways. First, by giving us clear
knowledge of the right in his plain and unmis-
takable precepts, and most of all in the beauty of
holiness as exhibited in his life; and, secondly,
by the irresistible motives to duty which he
supplies."

The only reason why I am bound to do anything is because it is intrinsically right and fitting.
Purity, industry, charity, reverence for all that
is great, love for all that is good, are enjoined
upon me by the law of my nature.

Thus we are led to see the reasonableness of
the requirements of love to God, while at the
same time the nature of that love is made apparent. For love to God is reverence toward and
communion with the All-Perfect. We have affection for human companions; it is natural for us
to feel admiration for the works of genius and for
the glorious universe itself, where beauty is an
all-pervading presence. How natural, therefore,
that we should revere and commune with the
infinite Spirit in whose image our human friends

are created, of whose wisdom, power, and goodness all outward things are but the expression
and revelation !

Who, then, in the light of such facts, can see
in this great commandment other than a blessed
privilege ? The wonder is that any one who believes in God, and in such a God as is revealed in
Christ, can fail to fall upon his knees and adore.

There are those to-day who tell us that waiv-
ing, for the time, the question of the existence of
a Divine wisdom and power, it is apparent that,
whether such a being is in the universe or not,
conscious communion with, and love for him, find-
ing its expression in worship, is an impossibility —
an indication of an imperfect condition in human
development. This was the philosophy of August
Comte. Some of his recent disciples boldly assert that the day is drawing near when no spires
shall pierce the sky, and men shall no longer
wrestle with the invisible, like Jacob, seeking and
obtaining a blessing. The time and money devoted
to such purposes will hereafter, it is asserted, be
given to altruistic schemes for the improvement
of humanity, and the churches will be converted
into schools of technology, gymnasiums, theatres,
and bureaus of scientific charity.

Our attention is frequently called in confirmation of this position to the break between modern thought and faith, to the alienation of culture and the hard-working classes from the church, and to a so-called irreconcilable conflict between science and religion. A traveller comments upon the fact that the beautiful and costly St. Patrick's Cathedral in Dublin is used only for religious services, which go on almost without interruption, day and night. But the great church stands in the midst of a population sunken in poverty and vice, constantly disturbing its ceremonies with the pathetic cry for daily bread, to which, apparently, the priest at the altar turns a deaf ear, as he swings his censer and chants his prayer. And so it is said by some, the institution of worship exists in a suffering and needy world to-day a useless and extravagant custom, which hardens men's hearts to the real needs of society, and might better give place to the more practical " worship of humanity," that is, the effort to elevate and improve " the outward condition of the other half."

But these criticisms are all superficial. They ignore one of the deepest needs of human nature

—communion with the Perfect. Man *must* worship. The commandment to love God is not only privilege but prophecy. "We are created for thee," says St. Augustine, "and we can find no rest until we rest in thee." When wonder dies, and awe exists no longer in the human mind, when the sense of mystery and dependence fades away, when man becomes less than man, then will he cease to look above himself. Knowledge only deepens reverence, and leads us to say, "O God, thou art our refuge in all generations!"

So worship, the expression of love toward God, is as natural and necessary as faith in him is reasonable. It must be admitted, however, that it is possible to live, for a time, in neglect of this supreme privilege; indeed, it is one of the perils of our day and generation.

The absorption in things outward and temporal, the tendency to discuss "every new thing" purely from the intellectual standpoint, and the low ideals of life and conduct so common among large classes of people, blind the eyes of thousands to the real needs of humanity. No longer held in the church by the belief that future happiness is some-

how secured by this alliance, the multitudes have
followed false leaders, and, like the Jews of old,
deserting the temple of their fathers, have turned
to their idols. The situation is serious; for where
there is no open vision, the people perish. There
is but one consolation, it must be temporary.
Driven back by want and woe, the world, like
the prodigal in the parable, will at length, through
very starvation, "arise and go to the Father."

Meanwhile, how plain is the duty of those
who see the obligations involved in religious faith.
With sincere spiritual worship they should hold
forth the word of truth, not driven but drawn
to the sweet old ways of communion; saying
ever with the Psalmist, "A day in thy courts is
better than a thousand. I had rather be a door-
keeper in the house of my God than to dwell
in the tents of wickedness," and so realizing,
within their own experience, the truth of the
beautiful words of Faber, —

> " I worship thee, sweet will of God,
>   And all thy ways adore;
>   And every day I live, I seem
>   To love thee more and more."

The power of human influence is subtle and

far-reaching; and the hardest blow we can give the arrogant scepticism that would cheat our fellow-men out of the noblest possession of the soul — adoring love to God — is to be steadfast and unmovable, worshipping him who is a Spirit "in spirit and in truth." What blessed results in character grow out of the faithful observance of this obligation! By the altar of our prayers we spontaneously cast away every lingering compromise with sin. False words, fraudulent acts, cruel revenge, guilty relations with our fellow-creatures, — these pass from the soul animated with love towards God. And in their place comes a holy consecration to the true, the beautiful, and the good, pervading the heart with happiness and praise, as the skylark fills the heavens with his glad song. Moreover, it is in the reception of this obligation of religion that we are led directly to the recognition of all those duties to our fellow-men which some thinkers assure us should supplant the adoring love of the soul toward its Creator. In our love to God we find the noblest motive for the second great obligation of religion — love toward man. We are all the children of an infinite Father, and derive our being and nature from him, and, therefore, "all ye are brethren." For us to say that we love God, and at the same time to hate and destroy our fellow-men, or even to be indifferent to their welfare, would be an absurdity. "He that loveth not his brother whom he hath seen, how can he love God whom he hath not seen?" The fact is that religion has never been satisfied with raising temples of worship, but has belted the earth with kindly charities. Wherever men have worshipped a compassionate Father, they have become compassionate in turn to their fellow-creatures. Jesus taught that the first duty of man is to love the Lord our God; but he added, as though it were a logical conclusion, "and thy neighbor as thyself." Moreover, in his example, whose whole life was spent in a conscious walk with God, we have a supreme ideal of the noblest and strongest love for man, — a love that knew no bounds of nationality, clime, or worth, sought everywhere the welfare and happiness of humanity, was as impartial and as changeless as the eternal goodness itself. This divine compassion for man manifested itself in parables, like that of the good Samaritan, which are read with as untiring interest to-day as when written, two thousand years ago. It found expression in deeds of mercy that have won the world, and moved his followers to do works greater than miracles for the amelioration of the suffering, the helpless, the degraded, and the sinful.

Truly, though the form was old, the spirit was new in those ever memorable words of his, "A new commandment I give unto you, that ye love one another, as I have loved you." This last clause transformed the love of man from a sentiment to a principle.

The love which the world practised was as the shallow mountain stream to the bottomless ocean surrounding the globe, when compared to the Divine compassion which Jesus illustrated in his teachings and example; and this spirit is an obligation of religion incumbent upon every one who has heard and obeyed his summons, who said, "Follow me." It is the test of discipleship.

What a transformation would the recognition of such a duty, and its universal practice, effect in human society! What must become of every debasing trade, of every immoral custom, that injures or degrades our fellow-man, in the light of this principle? So-called Christian nations would hardly send forth vessels to the heathen with missionaries on the deck and rum in the hold. It would not be necessary to reveal to an astonished world the extent of the opium trade between Christian England and heathen China. Protests would be unnecessary against the publication of immoral literature; while the relations of capital and labor, and the problems of dealing with the criminal classes, would find speedy settlement if men accepted the sentiment of the apostle, " in honor preferring one another."

Christian nations bearing upon their banners the cross of Christ, the supreme expression of love to man, would hardly find it consistent to deplete Europe of her best young life that their standing armies might be maintained in idleness; or to tax the poor to the point of despair for the support of a useless and oftentimes degenerate nobility.

Instead of lamenting our small navy, it would be counted the glory of America that she had passed the need of such relics of barbarism, save for commercial purposes or as illustrations of human progress in scientific knowledge. Love to man like this, would suggest better methods for the settlement of national questions than the terrible destruction and the cruel and widespread sufferings produced by war and bloody persecutions, of which, alas! we have illustrations in this end of the century. Our prisons would become workshops and schools, where, by severe discipline, the criminal, never deprived of hope, should, through a righteous punishment, involving wholesome instruction, arise to self-respecting manhood.

The poor would find — what they need more than money — friends to redeem them from their poverty; while strikes and labor-wars would disappear when the law of love moved the employer to justice, and the employee to faithfulness.

Think, too, what transforming influence would be felt in the more private relations of life! The stability of the home would be secured; and many, governed by principle where now passion rules, would remain faithful to the solemn vows made at the altar — vows so often lightly broken, and bringing with sad and increasing frequency such unholy results into many a desolate dwelling.

After all, the question in society is not so much whether we shall have a severe or liberal law of divorce, as whether men shall recognize the fact that true love is not hateful lust, but a changeless and unselfish devotion to the welfare of its objects.

Dr. Ware writes delightfully of the *Compromises of Love.* Happy, thrice happy will be our homes, happy the children, now so often more unfortunate than if deprived by death of parental care, when men learn the meaning of that phrase!

Love to man will lead to the only toleration worth the name; that is, a sincere respect for the honest opinion of our neighbor, and the recognition of the fact that all who are seeking the truth are our fellow-laborers, and are the instruments as truly as ourselves in the hands of divine Providence for bringing about the answer to the world's prayer, "Thy kingdom come."

It is said that "the world has outgrown Christ and his religion." Outgrown Christ! When we compare the actual condition of society with the ideals suggested to our minds by his law of love, how apparent it is that we have not yet touched the hem of his garment!

Dean Stanley tells of an old Scotch Methodist who in his earlier years had clung vehemently to one or the other of two small sects on either side of the street. " The street I am now travelling in, lad, has nae sides; and if power were given me, I would preach purity of life more, and purity of doctrine less, than I did." — " Are you not a little heretical in your old age?" said his interlocutor. " I care na'. Names have not the same terror on me they once had, and since I have grown old, I have had whisperings of the still small voice that the footfalls of faith and their wranglings will never be heard in the Lord's kingdom whereunto I am nearing; and, as love cements all differences, I'll perhaps find the place roomier than I thought in times by past."

Thus are we led to see what gracious privileges are involved in our religious faith, as we stand in the sunlight of that interpretation of Christianity which leads us, in the spirit of Christ, to call God our Father, and to say of our brother man, " O God, I can trust for the human soul." May we also learn that this Christian optimism leads not to indifference. It is instead a most strict and solemn standard of duty, teaching us that there is "no substitute" for purity of heart and uprightness of life. It is the will of God that his kingdom should come upon earth, and that "all men should be saved, and come to a knowledge of the truth;" yet this divine purpose will be realized in this world or any other realm of being only when each child of God is imbued with a profound sense of the obligations of religion. For the prayers and adoration of his children return from the bosom of God to the hearts of men, transformed into gracious and changeless purposes for the redemption of humanity, even as the mists of the mighty cataract, thundering in its solitudes, rise to the skies only to come back with fructifying power to the earth again. In the language of Ralph Waldo Emerson, "This great, overgrown, dead Christianity of ours still keeps alive, at least, the name of a Lover of mankind. But one day all men will be lovers, and every calamity will be dissolved in the universal sunshine," — the day when all men worship the Lord in the beauty of holiness.

SAVED BY CHRIST.

GIDEON ISAAC KEIRN.

SAVED BY CHRIST.

WHEN the advent of Jesus was announced, the angel said to Joseph, "It is he that shall save his people from their sins." It is of this saving power of Jesus, of his work in the human heart, of him as "the Word made flesh" and dwelling among men, and of him as the life and energy of the soul, leading it to God, that I am to write. The subject is a practical one. I am to have in mind the man or woman engaged in the cares of life; therefore the purely theological or controversial will, so far as possible, be avoided. Yet, since the theme is Christ as a Saviour of the individual soul, any doctrine germane to the subject must of necessity be practical.

I. *Saved by the Power of Christ's Personality.*

The human mind is so constituted that it is most effectually moved by personality. An abstract truth or theory will have an effect upon any mind which comprehends it; but the most effectual means of giving it possession of the mind is through some person in whom the truth dwells as a moving power. The most efficient agent for bringing about a reform is not a list of written precepts upon the subject, but those precepts embodied in a warm heart. We often hear men say of certain wrongs that they will right themselves, or that certain difficulties will " take care of themselves." The truth is, they never did take care of themselves, and they never will. They have always been taken care of by personal sacrifice. William of Orange took care of the oppression of Holland; Martin Luther, of the Reformation; Channing, Murray, and Ballou, of the more liberal ideas of God and the brighter destiny of the human race. The same has been true of every reform, from the most ancient to the most recent. Mighty truths must have mighty souls to voice them in word and life before the world can comprehend them. All the greatest and best principles of our modern civilization have been paid for in the coin of personal effort and sacrifice. Such is the law of human progress.

It is through the operation of this law that

Christ has had such a marvellous effect upon the world, and has saved every soul whom he has saved. It is through this law that he will continue to work until he hath drawn all men unto himself. Perhaps nearly all his truths had been taught in some form before he came; but they never took hold of the world as they did when he taught them. The reason of this is that when he once taught a truth it was ever afterward imbued with his personality. He never wrote a gospel; but the truths of the gospel he taught were so intimately and vitally a part of himself, and he so impressed his life upon his followers, that wherever his teachings go in his name somehow his personality goes with them. It is a marvellous fact that he vitalizes his word with a subtle influence, with an individuality, a magnetism, a something which no one can describe, but which everyone recognizes, a something which cannot be taken from it because it is an essential part, and which gives it its power over the human soul. It is Christ, and not his truth only, that moves us.

Thus in all the duties and struggles of everyday life we have the help of his inspiration. The man under temptation finds an example of resistance and a help to victory in the forty days in the wilderness. The selfish heart finds its selfishness rebuked and ultimately destroyed by the life of Christ, for he teaches brotherly love as much by deed as by word. The man prone to revenge learns from him to forgive his brother, " not until seven times seven, but until seventy times seven." All other teaching of forgiveness pales before his own act in his dying hour. Who can, in thoughtful imagination, sit at the foot of the cross and witness the awful cruelty of his enemies, and hear in the moment of his greatest agony his prayer, " Father, forgive them," and not turn away ashamed of his own unrelenting disposition. Perhaps we feel that the most difficult thing for us to do is to love our enemies. Here again Jesus asks only what he himself did from the beginning. He loved his friends and loved them tenderly; but he loved his enemies also. He saw in them something more than an enemy, something more than bigotry and sin ; he saw a brother, a child of God, a possible saint.

Such examples, which might be extended to almost any length, are sufficient to show the close personal relation between the sayings and the life of Christ, that he not only taught us what to do, but showed us how to do it.

> " When Jesus, our great Master, came
>   To teach us in his Father's name,
>   In every act, in every thought,
>   He lived the precepts which he taught."

In Jesus we have not only an example, but a perfect example ; far above us, it is true, but the more helpful on that account, because a man can best shape his character only in comparison with a perfect model. A recent writer says, in illustration of this thought, that the most skilful wood-carver, working with the greatest care, cannot make his second copy from his first, his third from his second, and so on to a large number of copies, lest in his last production he would not recognize his original model, because he had successively copied his unconscious errors. He must always have his model before him, and work from that. If this is true in the material and the seen, how much more is it true in the spiritual and the unseen, which enter into the formation of character. Man must have constantly before him a faultless model by which to work, else human defects will be unrecognized. Christ is himself that much needed model, that perfect example in all things, by which we may shape our characters, causing them to grow more and more like him who was " without sin." As Elizabeth Channing has so finely said, " By his life he set the most perfect example of goodness that man can conceive, reverent and obedient as a child, in maturity a model of active and passive virtue. Awake to the sinfulness of sin and faithfully warning of its deformity, he loved the sinner and labored for his salvation. He went about doing good, but observed meditation and prayer. In his character, he was free from earthly ambition, and steadily aspired to spiritual perfection. His trust in his divine Father was as complete as his sympathy for his human brother. His pity for his enemies equalled his love for his friends."

Some one may ask, " Does not Christ save us by his death ? " Only in the same way that he saves us by his life. That which is generally known as Christ's atonement is a result, and not a process. Atonement is at-one-ment. It means a state of harmony, or union with God. This is the result of all that Christ did, both in his life

and in his death. There is no magic or mystery
in his death which makes it the all of his saving
power; but there is a much needed help and example to be found in the way in which he bore
the suffering and trials of the last day of his life.
If there is one thing that the world needs to-day
more than anything else, it is a loyalty to conviction, and a revival of the sense of duty and
moral responsibility. There is a large class of
people who live as though they thought they
were to consult only their pleasure and con-
venience in assuming the responsibilities of life.
The call of duty is unknown to them. The voice
of pleasure is the only voice they hear. They
are loyal to so much of truth as will cost them
nothing, or so much as every one else believes.
If, perchance, God gives them a higher truth,
they hide it under a bushel lest they lose some
of their popularity, if it be known that they
possess it. Many people who think themselves
saved by the death or " the blood " of Christ are
fallen into this very sin, from which his death
was designed to save them. He could have been
popular had he chosen to be disloyal, and live
as though it mattered not what he believed, or

where he cast his influence. He could have
escaped suffering had he chosen to run away
from duty. Had he done this, he would not
have been a complete Saviour, for he would have
encouraged that sin from which our day and generation is suffering so much. He chose rather
to be loyal to his convictions, though it cost
him his life. He felt a deep moral responsibility. He knew that he owed it to his Father
to be faithful to the highest which He had given
him, and trust the result to His infinite love.
How much of the saving power of Christ's death
the world has lost because it has been looking
to it for something which it does not contain,
and because it has failed to see that which is
really there! If, instead of seeking the mysterious, men had only looked to Calvary for the
highest manifestations of a simple, faithful, brave
adherence to truth and the call of duty, which
is the voice of God, we would have been a
braver and stronger people than we are; we
would have been more ready to bear moral responsibilities, and the highest truths would have
been more generally established. Every man who
comes thoroughly to know, with mind and heart,

the calm, loyal, victorious Jesus under trial, will be led by him to victory.

In this capacity of teacher, example, and personal embodiment of divine life, Jesus becomes our Saviour from sin. To the sinner who compares himself with the immaculate he brings conviction; then his attitude toward the convicted is a strong and tender admonition to forsake sin; then, when the resolution to forsake sin is made, that is, when the man is converted, Jesus, by the marvellous fulness of his life, imparts power to walk in the better way; for every one who will ask himself, "What would Christ do were he in my place?" will find, if sufficiently familiar with his life, just the word or deed that will help him. No one ever was, and no one ever will be, placed in circumstances involving principles which were not involved in something that Christ said or did. Not that he performed the outward acts which we are to perform, not that we are to do at all times the deeds done by him, nor that we are necessarily to use the ceremonies and ritual of his time; but in the life he lived in his day and age of the world, and with the people of his time, he exemplified every principle which we are called upon to use in our time, applied to our affairs. This is the work of the Saviour under the divine law of personality; it is the touch of Christ upon the soul of man, bidding it be clean and strong.

II. *Saved by Christ's Revelation.*

Christ saves by revealing that which the world could not otherwise know, or could not have known so soon as it did, had it not been for his revelation. He reveals the character of God. It is impossible for man, by any help whatsoever, fully to know God. It is difficult for him to form even a helpful idea of a Being so vast; and yet it is indispensable to his best living that he should have some understanding of the character of his Creator. Ignorance of God, or wrong ideas of him, have held man in bondage to doubt, fear, and superstition, and have made a tyrant of him who otherwise would have been a brother. It is possible for a man without a belief in God to live a good life; but it is impossible for him to live as good a life as he could had he a realizing sense of the Father. And yet, indispensable as this knowledge is to the best living, man must have some help in order that he obtain it in any

satisfactory measure. Left to himself, he is lost
in his own abstractions and errors. If all the elements in the character of the Infinite could be
combined in miniature in one person, it would be
possible for our little minds to comprehend that
person, and so know enough of God to meet the
soul's practical need. Such a person would serve
as a picture in which we might see the nature and
disposition of the Infinite. We have this much
needed miniature, this picture of God (I speak
reverently), in Christ. He came as a representa-
tive of God, not representing His greatness, for
that would be impossible, but His goodness or the
quality of His character. This he so well portrays
that he could say, " He that hath seen me, hath
seen the Father." That is, he who thoroughly
knows Christ has been led through him to know
the character of God. To know one's character is
to know that person. " The conception of God
has been spiritualized through the teachings of
Jesus. He is no longer to the believing soul
mere will, intellect, or holiness ; He is not force,
power, or law. He is one like ourselves ; a friend
to whom we can go, whom we can lean upon; a
master who teaches us the word of life ; a loving

heart that trusts us and is trusted by us. He turns not from us when we forget Him, but grows even more anxious for our good, if that is possible. Though we forget Him and revile Him, and will have none of His love, yet He loves on and will never forsake us. It has thus come about that the thought of God is winning, attractive, uplifting." In Christ God makes a unique approach to man, and brings so much of himself within man's perception as it is possible for him to comprehend. Jesus thus becomes a revelator, disclosing that which the world did not know, and that which we have no right to say it ever could have known in its tenderness and fulness without such revelation.

Christ's revelation saves from weakness. Man is made to feel that he is not left to depend upon himself alone. He is made to know that infinite wisdom, power, and love, which know no failure, will sustain him, and consequently he is filled with hope. The wounded soldier on the field of battle is faint and weary, and feels that he must die. Just as he is about to fall out of the ranks he hears the cry of victory shouted back from the front. It fills him with new courage and strength.

He forgets his fatigue, forgets his wounds, and presses forward that he too may participate in the victory. So with the soldier in life's battle. He is wounded and sin-stained and faint, and feels that he can do no more, when, from the Captain of salvation, he hears sounded back from the distant future the cry of " Victory, victory to the hosts of God, victory, for ' God is all in all.' " It gives him new courage, new power; he presses forward that he may participate in the final and eternal triumph of righteousness. This bright and victorious end Christ declares when he says, " And I, if I be lifted up from the earth, will draw all men unto me ; " when he says, " There shall be one fold and one shepherd ; " when he enunciates the parable of the lost sheep and the lost piece of money ; and, in fact, whenever he tells of the all-conquering love of the Father. To think of God as Creator may cause one to wonder at his power and resources ; to think of him as Judge *only,* may cause one to tremble before his throne ; but to think of him as a loving Father who will *reach after* his children and ultimately *induce* them all to come home, is to have one's love, and all that is good within one, stirred and brought to life in response to the love and goodness enthroned above. When the world comes to know this, it will be saved from despair and weakness, and will be filled with joy and hope.

As revelator Jesus saves from overwhelming sorrow. To one beset with " living trouble " he shows that the value of existence is not to be measured by the amount of its gladness or sadness, but by the life of the soul, God's greatest gift, which is back of all joy and sorrow. Having this in abundance, man can lose other blessings, if he must, and still feel that the greater and better part remains. Every faithful Christian comes to feel as one of the first and perhaps the greatest Christian felt, that " our light affliction, which is but for a moment, worketh for us a far more exceeding and eternal weight of glory; while we look not at the things that are seen, but at the things that are not seen." A lady of beautiful Christian spirit, who had been under very great trial, once said to me, " I would not for the world again go through with what I have undergone; and yet, somehow, now that I have passed through it, I would not for the world be without it; for I have approached nearer than ever before to my Saviour and my God, and they have given me blessings which it seems to me I could never otherwise have received, and which are the most precious treasures I possess." She simply realized the truth of what Paul says in his words just quoted. She had received the blessing Christ promises to all the weary and heavy-laden that come unto him.

When death comes Jesus destroys it by bringing life and immortality to light, and causes it to lose its former dread significance, and to take its place as only one incident in the continuous life which begins with birth and lasts forever. To such as receive from him this faith in its fulness, there can be no anxiety about those who have passed on, nor any doubt about meeting them in the future, for the promises which Jesus makes are assured to us by no less than infinite power. They hear them as the voice of God speaking through His Son. The tender words of comfort spoken to the apostles in their sorrowing hour are spoken alike to all: "Let not your heart be troubled: ye believe in God, believe also in me. In my Father's house are many mansions : if it were not so, I would have told you. I go to prepare a place for you. And if I go and prepare a place for you, I will come again, and receive you unto myself; that where I am, there ye may be also." He who thoroughly believes in Jesus and these blessed promises can never be overthrown by any possible calamity or sorrow, but in spite of all will have a peace which surpasses his own understanding, and which Jesus gives, not "as the world gives," but as he alone can give.

The child born into this world is confronted with the unknown and mysterious as soon as its intelligence begins to take cognizance of its surroundings. It asks its elders and parents puzzling questions. They stand to it in the relation of interpreters of —

"The meaning hid life's common things beneath."

These mysteries do not all vanish with increasing years and intelligence. Some of them even grow deeper and more profound. Man asks, " Why suffering? Why ignorance? Why is sin allowed? What is man? What his destiny? "

Many have been thrown into doubt and darkness because they could not satisfactorily answer these and other equally perplexing questions. They need an interpreter, some one who can at least give a key by the aid of which the answer may be discovered. Jesus is that interpreter. He shows us manhood as it is to be when its growth and development are complete. He answers our question, " What is man ? " by teaching that he is a child of God, a brother of himself, and hence possessing a nature similar to his own, and capable of results like those we see in him. He explains and exalts manhood by setting it before us in its ideal form. He who sees in Jesus that which represents what God designs that he himself shall be when the divine work is completed in his soul, can never be troubled about the value or meaning of life, even though it is beset by heavy burdens and severe trials. He even explains these burdens and trials; he interprets the ignorance and mistakes and sins of life by showing them to be the struggles of imperfection toward designed perfection, of impurity toward designed purity. He makes all these things plainer by revealing the ideal man-

hood in which they are to result. He interprets
to each man his life by revealing to him its
nature, its aims, and its possibilities. The man
who finds his own life explained in the greater
and fuller life of Jesus, finds likewise every other
man's life so explained, since every other man is
his brother, under the same Providence, and of
similar nature and destiny. He interprets the
future by showing it to be but the enlarged
and purified present. As we have already seen,
he is the great interpreter of the doings and
purposes of God. When he declares the universal brotherhood of man, the universal Fatherhood of God, the universal immortality of the
soul, the final, universal triumph of good over
evil, he throws an inextinguishable flood of light
on life's dark places. Jesus, *life's interpreter*, is
indeed " the light of the world."

He does not give us the interpretation, written
page by page and word by word; but, what is
better, he indicates the direction wherein, with
faith and wisdom for his guide, man may ultimately reach the plain and satisfactory end. He
is himself the great luminary of the way, the guiding star by which the soul may confidently pursue

its course in search of truth and peace and life. When Jesus reveals the unconquering love which rules the universe, he reveals the key by which, and by which alone, all life's mysteries may be solved. I could not know these things as I know them now, were it not for him; he is therefore my Saviour, because he is my revelator. Phillips Brooks says, " Christ's redemption of the world means, for each man who believes it, just these three things: the revelation to man of his own value, the value of his fellow-man, and the nearness and dearness of God." The man who practically knows this is lifted above his fears and doubts.

III. *Salvation above Salvation from Sin.*

The saving power of Christ does not end here. To save a man from sin and every moral evil is a work marvellously great. Our hearts gladly cry out that it is sufficient to give him a "name which is above every name." But, great as it is, there is a phase of his saving power which goes even farther. When we think of him as he lived on earth, he never seems to us as merely a sinless man. He was more than this, much more. There is a transcendent greatness on which our minds are fixed when we think of him. His soul had wrought itself through the realm of temptation into that of communion.

His prayers are the soul's earnest pleading, the child's confident talk with the Father. In their beautiful simplicity they confide in a Father's tenderness. With him there is no room for speculation or query about God; he does not simply have faith in Him, he seems to know Him as positively as he knew Peter and James and John. He knew that he could not be alone even in his hour of darkness, when the disciples forsook him, for the Father was with him. There was a union of his life with God which is always conscious of the divine presence and counsel and inspiration and love. As to the endless life of all his Father's children, that was no more to be questioned than that the sun shines. His soul was so full of life that he lived and moved in these great spiritual realities. When we come to know this fulness of Jesus, we realize how much less than this, and how far below it, is mere sinlessness. It is his mission to man to give him more than sinlessness. He say, "I came that ye might have life, and have it more abundantly." To be saved from sin is negative, but to be filled with life is positive. It is salvation above salvation from sin.

The followers of Christ will be led into this graduate salvation, into the more abundant life which he came to bring, and into the knowledge which results from it. The degree of such knowledge may depend upon many things; it may depend upon education and surroundings, or upon what one thinks he ought to see in life, but it will depend chiefly upon purity. The sinful soul is necessarily the blind soul. "Blessed are the pure in heart, for they shall see God." None of us is wholly pure, consequently none of us has an entirely clear spiritual vision. There are many, however, who are able to hear the first accents of the still small voice, and to understand something of its message. They have begun to know those truths which come by this means. The critic may tell them, if he will, that they do not know what they profess to know; and yet they do know it, despite the contrary opinion. The soul has various avenues of knowledge. The heart is one of them. In some things the heart is more reliable than the mind or the senses.

When the heart of man gives him a fact, the value of which it is better able to determine than any other faculty of his being, he should receive it with the same confidence that he would had it come through some other avenue. Man should feel that he knows this class of facts as really as he knows any other class. "The natural man receiveth not the things of the Spirit of God: for they are foolishness to him: neither can he know them, because they are spiritually discerned." They must be so discerned. The other faculties are incapable of clearly seeing them, and fully appreciating them. It is the man of abundant spiritual perception who penetrates them most deeply and knows them best, hence his opinion upon these things is the more likely to be correct. He has learned of his great spiritual teacher to look into the future, and to know the Father. This is the beginning of that larger life which Christ works in the heart of his follower. He leads him up out of the realm of temptation and conflict, through which he himself passed, into that of knowledge and communion.

But the end is not yet. As far as the eye of the spirit can penetrate, we see the Lamb of God leading the race of man on and on in purity and knowledge and love to higher and still higher degrees of perfection. The endless future grows brighter, richer, and happier. This conception elates my soul with hope, it stirs my being with power to achieve, it fills my heart with love and gratitude to my Saviour, it moves me to avow faithfulness in my discipleship. The mission of Christ does not end when he has saved the world from sin. He is its leader in the boundless fields of perfection. So far as we can know, he is to lead humanity on forever and forever.

I have tried to show the work of Christ in the soul of man; how by the power of his great personality he impresses the principles of righteousness, how he reveals the truth that makes us free, and finally, how he leads us into communion and accord with God and the eternal. No one knows better than I how inadequately this has been done, and to how small a portion of these great truths I have been able to give utterance. Their greatness and beauty would surpass a more facile pen. The devout soul may realize them, although it may not find words sufficient to express that reality. To any one who would know these things to their heart's content, let me, in conclusion, offer a few thoughts leading to their attainment.

In the first place, you cannot receive the life of a man whom you do not know. In order to be helped by Christ, you must know him. Is it any wonder that many receive so little from his religion, when they give him so little thought? Be a daily reader of his life; be familiar with it all, especially its greatest chapters; ponder much upon his choicest sayings; dwell with him at Nazareth, and look out with him from those native hills upon life, and feel his yearning to save the world in which he lived; go with him to his baptism, and there with him make your own consecration; hear him call his first disciples; go with him on his journey to Galilee, and stop at Jacob's well, and hear the conversation with the woman of Samaria; journey on to Nazareth, and enter the synagogue with his neighbors and kinsmen, and listen to the sermon from the text for his life, " The spirit of the Lord is upon me, because he hath anointed me to preach the gospel to the poor; he hath sent me to heal the broken-hearted, to preach deliverance to the captive, and

recovering of sight to the blind, to set at liberty
them that are bruised, and to preach the acceptable year of the Lord;" dwell with him in his
Capernaum home; sail with him the Sea of Galilee, and listen to his parables and sermons from
nature; go with him on his missionary journeys,
and behold him touch the diseased with health,
and the dead with life; then turn with him
towards Jerusalem to celebrate his last Passover;
after the busy days in the Temple, go out on
the evenings of that marvellous final week of
his life to Bethany, and, surrounded with loving
friends, enjoy a quiet rest in that peaceful village
home; when you are purest in heart, enter that
holy of holies, the upper room, and sit with him
and his disciples at the last supper, and listen
to his tender parting words; then, purified still
more by this sacred experience, you may go with
him to dark Gethsemane, and standing apart, may
weep with him in his deep anguish, and witness
him returning serene and courageous. After this
you will not be surprised at his calmness in the
judgment hall, and will be prepared for his
victory on Calvary, and can with sympathy enter
into his transcendent glory on the resurrection

morn. Make his life from the manger to the ascension an open book, familiar in every word and deed, cherished in all its beauty. Know him, and you shall be known of him.

In the second place, when you have thus lived with Christ and become acquainted with him, when you have seen that his religion was life, and that he came not so much to teach a new theology as to live a new life, in a word, when you have seen what he was, be like him. Be the new husband and father, the new wife and mother, the new son or daughter, the new brother or sister, the new business man, the new ruler, the new man or woman in any sphere, which he would have you be. Like him make all things divine because they are done for God and to God, and not as unto men alone. When he says to you, "Love your enemies," do it. When he asks you to deny yourself, and take up your cross and follow him, obey, no matter how heavy that cross may be. All along your life, when he calls you to service, be quick to heed and faithful to fulfil.

Finally, you have seen, as you have followed him, how often Christ went away to pray, how earnestly he prayed for his disciples and himself, what an inexhaustible source of power this was to him, and how his life was transfigured by prayer. If this great strong personality must have frequent recourse to prayer in order to be sustained, much more must we. If he could not do without this help, how much less can we who are weaker than he. Let deep, earnest, simple prayer be thy daily habit; for if " in his name," that is, in his spirit, ye ask, " it shall be given unto you."

Who can say that Christ does not still actively and personally help his followers? When he was about to depart he assured the disciples that he would be with them after he had gone away; that is, after he had finally withdrawn his visible presence from them. There is no reason to think that it was possible for him to be with *them*, and is not now possible for him to be with *us*. They were men as we are men, and, when he had gone away, were related to him as his faithful followers are related to him to-day. There is, therefore, no reason to think that this promise was for them alone. We know that he is with us in the mighty uplift and marvellous inspiration of his great historic personality as recorded in the Gospels; but is he not with us even now in a still closer and more vital personal, soul-to-soul relation? The thought may be beyond us, we may not be able to see how it is, and yet he who never failed in any promise hath promised it. We may then feel assured that we can even now come into a spiritual meeting with the personal Jesus, and that he may touch and quicken us with new life and strength. Blessed privilege, sacred help! to look up to him, and feel that he is speaking to *us* when he says, " *Lo, I am with you alway, even unto the end of the world.*"

CHRISTIAN PEACE.

HARRISON SPOFFORD WHITMAN.

CHRISTIAN PEACE.

MANY years ago, a little vessel might have been seen, with sails spread, making across the dark Sea of Galilee. There were but a handful of men. One of them, reclining in the stern of the boat, was fast asleep. The others were beginning to cast anxious looks upon the black leaden clouds piling up so ominously from every side. It is but five miles across to the lonely deserted region on the eastern shore whither they were journeying. They were girt in with rugged hills and towering peaks. And before them these desolate hills, without a visible habitation or a single tree, rose abruptly from the water over a thousand feet.

Suddenly the storm that had been gathering struck down upon this little band in all its fury. The waves, lashed by the tempest, beat about them with terrific force, rising every moment higher and higher. The danger was extreme.

213

Yet the sleeper slept on, unmindful of the storm, the tumult, and the terror. But now the angry waves were beginning to pour over into the vessel itself, threatening every moment to ingulf it. Then the disciples, almost beside themselves with fear, awoke him with piercing cries of wild excitement, " Lord ! Master ! save ! we perish ! " Thereupon the Master arose in the calm majesty of his strength ; and hushing the raging tumult in their souls with the quiet words, " Why so fearful, O ye of little faith ? " he looked out upon the tempestuous sea, and said, " Peace ! be still." And immediately the winds ceased, and there was a great calm.

It is refreshing to dwell upon this picture — Jesus, at a single word, calming the troubled sea. For in this occurrence, which was enacted of old on the Sea of Galilee, we have a visible representation of the wonderful power which the Son of man exercises over the souls of men in all ages since. He stilled the raging waters. He spoke ; and the sea was at rest, hushed into stillness and peace. So does he calm the troubled soul. That " voice of a Saviour heard across the long generations can calm wilder storms than ever buffeted into fury the bosom of the inland lake."

Now, what is the secret of Christ's power? How is it that he is able to send peace into the human soul? And what is the nature of this peace which he imparts?

It may help to a clear understanding of this whole matter if we turn to the life of Jesus in its calm serenity. That life was pre-eminently a life of deep, unalloyed peace. It was not that he was exempt from temptation. He was tempted in all points as we are tempted. It was not that he was exempt from trial and suffering. He was " a man of sorrows and acquainted with grief." He knew, from personal experience, all about the hardships of life, — deprivation, want, weary toil. Often he had not where to lay his head. He was " despised and rejected of men." He encountered the fiercest of opposition. He was maligned and misrepresented, pursued even unto death by the cruel hate of bitter enemies. And in the darkest hour he was deserted by his friends, and left to bear his burden alone. Yet, in spite of all these untoward circumstances, one cannot fail to be impressed with the deep, abiding peace which characterized his whole life. There was no emergency so great or so sudden as to betray him unto undue agitation. When awakened suddenly from deep sleep at night by shrieking cries of fear, with the wild wind howling, and the waves breaking over him, he was yet calm, and evinced no sign of alarm. So in all the exigencies of his life. How the strife of men raged all about him! But with what composure did he bear himself through it all! It was the composure of absolute strength and absolute trust. There is no trace of anxiety or distraction or perturbation in all his life, in any word, act, or attitude, not even in that last scene in the divine tragedy, when, betrayed and deserted by his friends, when, mocked and scourged and crucified by his enemies, he hung bleeding upon the cross. As Dr. Fairbairn says, "While human passions were darkening Christ's path, and human enmities were preparing the doom that was to be his glory, sweet peace sat like the blessed angel of God within his spirit, and filled it with celestial light and joy." Not all the beating and tossing of the world of humanity could shake the serenity of his soul. His life reached up so completely into the Father's life, he found such perfect security and assurance in the ever present nearness and love of the Father, that he could but be profoundly at peace amid all the strife and turmoil of a wild, tempestuous world.

This peace which Jesus possessed he promised, as a precious legacy, to his disciples. "Peace I leave with you, my peace I give unto you." And this peace divine has been a marked feature in the life of those choice spirits who have walked nearest to the Master in love, obedience, and trust.

Not many men have had more, in outward relations, to vex and harass the soul than the Apostle Paul. He was continually beset with hardship and opposition and persecution. But, in every hour of trial and suffering, his calm spirit mounted superior to outward circumstances in the tranquillity of deep peace. "I have learned," he said, " in whatsoever state I am, therewith to be content." And this spirit became a dominant characteristic of his life. He stood serene and calm in all those experiences which usually fill the soul with a tumult of fear and dread, — whether in prison at Philippi, his body all lacerated from a Roman scourging, or in Jerusalem facing a raging mob, or on the wild sea in extreme peril for fourteen days with shipwreck at last, or in Nero's prison-house in Rome awaiting execution. Evidently St. Paul had gained the secret of his Master's peace. His soul was anchored in God, and his life was a magnificent exemplification of those grand words of triumphant faith, " We know that all things work together for good to them that love God."

And what is true of the Apostle Paul is true of thousands of Christian disciples in all ages since. They have come into possession of the Master's peace, — an untroubled peace of soul amid life's deepest mysteries.

Now, what is the meaning of all this? How is it that Christ's dying promise of peace has been so literally and abundantly fulfilled?

Christ imparts peace, in the first place, by communicating a larger life, and delivering from the bondage of evil. That which, above all else, proves destructive to genuine peace of soul is inward discord, — the discord which springs from guilty deeds and a sinful life.

The Greeks personified the guilty conscience

by the three Furies. These are represented as
pursuing the perpetrators of wicked deeds up and
down the earth with whips and scorpions. The
conception is true to nature. The conscience
pursues the guilty person with avenging stripes
and torturing stings. It holds up before him
continually the memory of the black deed. "Behold," it cries in condemnation, "this is your
doing." The power of conscience to harrow the
soul is well portrayed in the self-accusing words
of Macbeth, "Will all great Neptune's ocean
wash this blood clean from my hand?" He realizes that there is no more peace for him. "Macbeth shall sleep no more!"

And even when conscience loses its first sting,
when it ceases to torture with its stern accusation,
there is yet no real peace for the soul. The last
state of Macbeth, when he had become hardened
in crime, evinces even deeper disquietude than
that which had marked his early guilt. "Out,
out, brief candle: life's but a walking shadow; a
poor player, that struts and frets his hour upon
the stage, and then is heard no more: it is a tale
told by an idiot, full of sound and fury, signifying
nothing."

There is no deliverance from the disquietude of guilt but by deliverance from the evil. The inward jangling and discord are caused by the transgression of God's law of right. There is no possible peace for the wicked till they turn from their evil, and learn to do well.

Sin, then, is the great arch-enemy of peace. So long as one does evil, or pursues an evil course of life, he is contending against his nature and against God. The very elements of the universe are set in array against him, and the stars in their courses fight against him. At the same time there is an irrepressible conflict within. The man's better nature — his true self — is irreversibly opposed to the evil. And there can be no real peace but by conquest of the evil. In seeming opposition to his character as Prince of peace, Jesus declared he came not to send peace, but a sword. That is, his principles of righteousness and truth could but incur the opposition of sin and error, and stir them up to fierce hate and terrific strife. This is equally true of the human soul, and leads to an inevitable conflict within. It is in vain to cry, " Peace, peace; when there is no peace." And there is only one way of gaining genuine peace, —

not by yielding to the evil, not by compromising with the evil, but by fighting the evil and conquering it. And then comes peace, "full of joy, without one throb of tumultuous passion, the prelude of the peace of a happier world." This is the peace which Jesus gives. It is by the influx of his life and love that we may find deliverance and peace. It is a radical peace. It accepts of no compromise. It goes to the root of every wrong, and conquers peace by routing evil in every form, and bringing in concord and harmony. As Ruskin says, "No peace was ever won from fate by subterfuge or agreement; no peace is ever in store for any of us, but that which we shall win by victory over shame or sin — victory over the sin that oppresses, as well as over that which corrupts."

More and more, as we come into nearness with the Saviour, and triumph over the evil that is within by growth in Christian character, will we experience of the deep peace which was never absent from the Lord, — the "peace of God which passeth all understanding," the peace of a soul at one with God in the unruffled calm of a pure and holy life.

In the second place, Christ leads the soul into
a state of peace by the faith which he communi-
cates. Next to sin, the greatest foe to peace is
doubt. We look out upon a transitory world.
Flowers bloom and decay. And the sweet flowers
of human life, to all outward appearance, are
quite as evanescent. Life is crowded with dark
mysteries. As we contemplate these mysteries,
as we meditate upon the awful facts of pain
and sin and death, as we think of the mysterious lines of blood and suffering which run
through all the twisted skein of created existences,
there is no relief for mind or heart except as our
poor human vision shall be supported by an
abiding trust in God. How great must be the
disquietude of that disbelief which recognizes no
Heavenly Father in all this bewildering maze of
things! To think the adjustments of this world,
the course of events and history, are not planned
and executed in love, with a purpose and end that
love can justify; to think that evil is as likely to
triumph ultimately as good; to think that immortality is but a dream, while this present earth-life
is our all, — this, indeed, were to lacerate the
soul, and destroy the very roots of peace. It was

to deliver from the disquietude of doubt that Christ came, revealing the Father. "We are all encircled by omnipotent love," his words and life declare. And so, "amid the events that bear us onward," we can look out upon the dark mysteries of life with the calm assurance and the serene faith that make for peace. The highest reason and the largest faith are blended in one to those who walk near the Saviour in sincerity, in obedience, in trust.

How many go through life heavily burdened with anxiety and grim forebodings! What solicitude and care and perplexity to vex the weary soul! To many, indeed, the future looms up black and drear. It is streaked with the doubts and fears that reach out from their own distrusting soul.

From all this there is one sure deliverance. It is to be found in the simple faith and absolute trust of the Saviour, — trust in God as the Sovereign of the world, trust in his supreme wisdom and goodness and love always to do that which is best, always to do that which is right. Come what may, we are in his hands. With this great conviction we are fortified against the evils and calamities of life. We may not be able to understand all; but in that we do not understand we may fall back on trust, — trust in God because of his illimitable wisdom and goodness. Without this trust we are in darkness in this world, with no ray of light except that from flitting stars. We are lost amid the sad perplexities of life. But with this trust, we may believe that all those things which so distress and worry, and with which we have nothing to do, are shaped for good. With all our boasted freedom, which is, indeed, sufficient to make us accountable, it is only in small part that we make our lives. They are made for us. There is an infinite Power compassing us around which even in the darkest features of life is working for our best good.

> " And I smiled to think God's greatness flowed around our
>   incompleteness, —
> Round our restlessness, his rest."

In all the tribulations and disappointments and sorrows of life, how may the anguished soul, tempest-tossed, be hushed into calm by that strong filial trust which will never let go the living God, — which looks out into the uncertain future with calm and tranquil vision, assured that God in his infinite wisdom and love and power will reign triumphantly for good.

This great universe, with all its titanic forces, is ruled and fashioned by that almighty power. The great world of humanity, with its throbbing life, its hopes and fears, its tumults and strife, its pain and grief, is ruled by that same mighty hand of power, — ruled in wisdom and ruled in love. We are not heaving about on a turbulent sea of discord and confusion. There are ripples of discord, to be sure, caused by man's disordered will, and eddies running counter to the divine will. But the great trend of humanity is ever forward toward its destined end. It is held by the almighty grasp. The eternal purposes are going forward in beautiful simplicity and order. The pain and the sorrow are but incidental to the progress. They must yet be left behind. They are but " the background of the pattern which the Eternal Mind is weaving on the clashing looms of life ; and he who looks with true insight already sees gleaming threads falling into shapes of beauty and of light."

There are, as we have seen, two primary causes

for human unrest, — inward discord and distrust of God. These two great foes to true peace — sin and doubt — are really the only things that can greatly affect the serenity of man. These have to do with the soul life within and its attitude toward God. And the remedy must be applied where the disease is, — to the inward life. It is Christ's life and truth that must be applied, to destroy the sin and the distrust, to expand the higher life of love and faith. This is the peace which Jesus gives. It is a real, substantial peace, an abiding peace, a satisfying peace, a peace which reaches down into the depths of the soul, and which outward circumstances cannot destroy.

Yet how many there are that greatly mistake in this matter. How many seem to think the greatest enemies to peace lie without rather than within. And so the great concern of their life is to remove the outward trial or want. It is a mistake. This is the peace which the world proposes to give, — to remove the outward burden, to free the soul from trouble, to surround it with the ease and comfort of luxury and wealth. This is the peace which the world promises. But this is not the peace of the Saviour. He says, " *My* peace I give unto you: not as the world giveth, give I unto you." It is not the outward circumstances that make or unmake our peace, but the inward state of the soul and its attitude toward God. If there be inward discord or distrust of God, one cannot be at peace, though everything without be in the highest degree propitious. Wherever he may be, and whatever his environment, he will yet carry with him his own self, with all the elements of unrest. So long as these remain, there will be no peace. Just as with the fever patient who tosses from side to side in the vain effort to find relief from the burning heat within.

Neither, on the other hand, if there be harmony within, if there be perfect confidence in God, can the most unfavorable circumstances greatly disturb the calm repose of the soul. The surface of the life may be moved and tossed; but below the surface there will be a life of peace which no circumstance can greatly mar.

Some of the sweetest and most tranquil souls have yet been beset with deep sorrow and severe trial. But amid all they have lived in calm confidence, with the peace of God in their hearts.

No one could come into their presence without feeling rested. Though the sun hid its face, and dark clouds folded them about, no chill night-damp came within to wither the bloom of love and trust; no storms could shake them from their faith; no waves could sweep them from the eternal Rock of Ages.

This is Christian peace, — the peace which Christ promises to give his disciples. It is harmony instead of "chaotic passions in jar and discord." It is acquiescence in the will of God. Once let the soul be moored in the divine life, and though sorrow, sickness, loss, tribulation, roll in upon it, yet may it rise into the broad empyreal atmosphere of eternal verities, and come into a realizing sense of God's mighty love.

> " Like a cradle, rocking, rocking,
>   Silent, peaceful, to and fro;
>   Like a mother's sweet looks dropping
>   On a little face below, —
>   Hangs the green earth, swinging, turning,
>   Jarless, noiseless, safe, and slow ;
>   Falls the light of God's face, bending
>   Down, and watching us below.
>
>   And as feeble babes that suffer,
>   Toss and cry, and will not rest,

Are the ones the tender mother
Holds the closest, loves the best ;
So when we are weak and wretched,
By our sins weighed down, distressed,
Then it is that God's great patience
Holds us closest, loves us best."

THE IMMORTAL LIFE.

JAMES MILFORD PAYSON.

THE IMMORTAL LIFE.

"IF a man die, shall he live again?" "This is the great question," wrote a friend of Emma Abbott shortly after the death of that queen of song. No question so generally and persistently pleads for reply. We sometimes think there are many who rarely lift their eyes beyond the earthly horizon, who are rarely disturbed by any question save how to win fortune or position or pleasure. But probably there is no one who does not often face the west, where the sun of life goes down, and question about the new day. We are travellers on a highway barred by a cloud-gate. Our poor human eyes can neither see through nor around nor over. Sooner or later it opens and closes upon all. The footsteps of those who walk in blessed companionship with us are hastened, and the impenetrable mists hide them from our longing sight. Strain our vision as we may, we get no glimpse of the vanished form. We call after

them through the darkness, but there comes back
no reply. Men may show no interest in the institutions of religion, neglect all religious service,
repudiate all faith; but the great question, Into
what does that cloud-gate open? can never be
wholly without interest to any one.

> " One question more than others all
>   From thoughtful minds implores reply ;
>   It is as breathed from star and pall,
>   What fate awaits us when we die ? "

It is the object of the present essay to offer
some suggestions in answer. Already there have
been numberless attempts at reply. A certain
writer says that " every considerate person in the
unnumbered successions that have preceded us
has, in his turn, confronted the same facts, engaged in the same inquiry." So far from pre-
suming to more certain knowledge than thousands
of others, the present writer does not hope to offer any word that has not often been expressed
before. But he feels justified in his essay by the
general longing for light, and the hope that an
additional witness may help some one to journey
toward the cloud-gate with more elastic step and
more cheerful face.

" What fate awaits us when we die ? " It is
a question to which a not uncommon philosophy
of our time does not make very satisfactory
answer. Materialism would shatter at one blow
the sublimest hope of the ages. It would make
the grandest vision that has inspired the human
soul but " the baseless fabric of a dream." It
says that fate awaits us when we die which
awaits all material life, — every organic form, the
tree, the flower, the body, — a return to dust.
Aristoxenus, a Greek philosopher of the fourth
century before Christ, likened the relation between body and soul to that between the harp
and its harmony. Does not this essentially illustrate materialism to-day? The soul is a result
of highly organized matter. The brain is a kind
of electric apparatus that throws off the sparks
of thought and feeling. Of course this doctrine
demands an absolute denial of a future life.
There is no defensible doctrine of immortality
except that which says that the human spirit cannot die. If the soul is but the melody of this
material instrument, then when the instrument is
destroyed the melody will cease forever. Or to
change the figure, if the soul is but the flame

of this lamp of the body, then when the lamp is broken, or the oil is all gone, the flame will go out, never to shine again.

If the mind results in any way from bodily organism, is it not surprising that it should be so superior to it? All adown history mind has been conquering matter. What is the progress of civilization but the subjugation of the material by the human spirit? The body has constantly to bow to the soul's regal sway. When the body would rest, the soul can force it to move on. When it would sleep, the soul can say to the eyelids, you must not close. Observe into what marvellous subjection the mind of a pianist brings her fingers. The hand becomes the instrument of immortal executions on canvas and in marble, in obedience to a thought. It is in no small degree true that the soul is a sculptor to whom the body is clay. In quite a measure, thought and feeling can disfigure and transfigure bodily form. They turn the face into a tablet, upon which to write the story of their selfishness, unkindness, and vice; or a mirror from which to reflect their aspirations, beauty, and sweetness. Can that which so masters bodily organism be a product of it?

Professor Fisk says that "The only thing which cerebral physiology tells us, when studied with the aid of molecular physics, is against the materialist so far as it goes. It tells us that, during the present life, although thought and feeling are always manifested in connection with a peculiar form of matter, yet by no possibility can thought and feeling be in any sense the products of matter." Another writer says that the foremost scientists declare that the bodily organism is inert without the influence of an agent external to itself, and quotes an eminent scientist as saying of the body that "it cannot change its state of motion nor rest without the influence of some force from without. True spontaneity of movement is, therefore, just as impossible to it as to what we call dead matter. So we are compelled to admit the existence of an exciting cause in the form of some force from without to give the initial impulse in all vital actions." That is, it is an agent independent of the body that animates and moves it. The brain does not produce thought. It is but the instrument of that which thinks. The relation of the body and soul is not that of the harp and its harmony, but of the harp and its player. The destruction of the harp does not injure the harper.

This doctrine that the real person, the being who thinks and feels and loves, survives the dissolution of the body, is confirmed in many ways. It is not without reason that the fact that the doctrine of immortality has ever been so nearly universal, has been regarded as strongly suggestive of its truth. A belief in immortality of some sort has been largely prevalent in all lands and ages. It has been prominent, at least, in most of the world's great religions. The religion of ancient Egypt had its Amenti, almost as real as the present world to the believer; the old Scandinavian its Valhalla, a splendid mansion in the skies, roofed with shields and supported by spears. The most widespread of all religions, Mohammedanism, owes its marvellous conquests very largely to its vivid doctrine of a future life. Though in crude form, it has been as surely the heritage of the savage as the civilized mind.

Sir John Lubbock declares that certain West Africans are entirely without the idea of a future life. But probably his statement is to be received with some caution. It is doubtful if there be any who have not some intimation of it, if it be no more than a belief in spirits haunting the abodes of the living. The Greenlander looks for an eternal summer-land beneath the ocean, or a paradise in the sky, where the Northern Lights reveal the sporting of happy souls. Some savages think the Milky Way the path to a celestial abode, white with journeying spirits.

Is not the fact of this sublime expectation being so generally and deeply rooted, especially in the primitive soul, a strong intimation that it is not a vain hope? Think how much antago-nism the unthoughtful mind has had to meet in its hope of a survival of death. Doubtless be-neath the surface of material nature, there is strong testimony to the immortal life. But that written on the surface, nature's only message to the unthoughtful, is against it. As you bend above the white and motionless face of a friend, what is there to indicate that he still lives? Is it not wonderful that the primitive mind, in con-stant association with death as the final goal of all, with no perception of any reason why it does not end all, should have conceived and cherished the belief that an eminent preacher has called "the most audacious that has ever entered into the imagination of man," that it is to live forever? Could the expectation have survived human experience had it been born of priestcraft or originated in dreams? Is it not a much more reasonable thought that the primal root of the belief in immortality is a kind of instinct, as surely indicating the existence of the life it suggests, as the instinct of the birds that of the southern home toward which in autumn it inspires them to wing their way?

Does not this hope of the endless life of the soul find further and very strong confirmation in the soul itself? Is there not written in the endowments of human nature very certain prophecy of their continuance? In his endowments, is not man out of all proportion to this brief life? Has he not been made too much of a being to live so short a time? He has been given a mind capable of comprehending the universe in no small degree; of transforming the world and itself; of enlisting the mightiest forces of nature into its service; of conceiving and executing that which lives through the centuries; of singing a song that thrills human hearts generations after the fingers that penned it are dust. Think of creating a being to so completely justify the saying, "Thou hast made him a little lower than the angels," to live but a little while at the longest, and often to be almost as fleeting as a shadow. Many a great intellect remains in this world barely long enough to show what it can do. Indeed, the light of many a great mind goes out in the cradle. If man has only this life, then in his creation God is like an artist who paints a great picture to adorn his studio but for a day, and then be cast as rubbish to the void, or spoiled before any one can enjoy looking at it; like a sculptor who exhausts his genius upon a statue that is soon to be broken in pieces. Infinite pains and great genius in the construction of a machine show that it was intended for more than the usefulness of a day. Does not the creative genius expressed in the human soul suggest that it was intended for more than this brief life?

And is not this further suggested in the soul's capacity for growth? If every person experienced life enough here to completely unfold all his powers, that would possibly suggest that this is all of life. But many are taken from the world before their intellectual and moral development really begins. Many more live barely long enough to begin such growth; and not very much more do those who enjoy the best opportunities of a long life. Here is a student who has spent three-score years in diligent explorations in a certain realm of thought. He is renowned for his intimate knowledge of his chosen field. Yet, as he sees how rapidly his sun is setting, his chief regret is that the night will call him from so unfinished a task. He says he knows but little compared to what he might know, give him time. Leonardo da Vinci was a marvel of intellectual culture. But how much more marvellous would have been his acquirements could he have lived until to-day? It must be intended that the soul shall fully unfold its powers. Under no circumstances can it do so in this life. Must it not have another life?

All this is further enforced by the fact that so many high ambitions and hopes fail of fulfilment here. There is the story of a young woman returning from a foreign land, weary, ill, longing for home, on a steamer burned in sight of the blessed goal. It illustrates much human experience. Death often compels the abandonment of great hopes on the eve of fruition. Are they never to be realized? How many persons, just as they are prepared to experience great good in life, are called to leave it! Is the good never to be attained? With much toil and pains young men and women are educated for usefulness and happiness. They cross the threshold with their hearts pulsating with great ambitions about what they are going to be and do. But at the very beginning the tools, fashioned with such care for carving out fortune, drop from their paralyzed hand. Are they never to be taken up again? Under the mysterious touch, the brush of the artist falls with the great picture as yet but an outline. Is the picture never to be finished? The voice of the poet is hushed with many a song yet unsung. Are those songs forever to remain unsung? Some of the most beautiful friendships in this world are blighted by death almost as soon at they have bloomed, while full of promise. Is that blessed association, upon which death so early intruded, every thought of which is a joy, henceforth to be only a brief memory?

The administration of the divine government is

equally suggestive of continuous life. While it may generally prove true here, that "Whatever a man soweth that shall he also reap," often it does not. Many of the world's greatest benefactors have lived to reap little more than persecution and suffering for their self-sacrificing toil; while those who constantly injure the world often flourish like the green bay-tree, perhaps to the evening time, and amid abundant comfort, seemingly at least, fall peacefully asleep. Many crimes are committed for which this world affords no chance for penalty. The soul often takes its flight with the fresh stains of sin yet upon it. And there is another respect in which the divine rule demands more than the present life. Doubtless there is less inequality in human lot than is often thought. Much called inequality is apparent rather than real. Yet some do have a much better chance for holiness and happiness in this world than others. If the divine rule is to justify itself, there must be experience with it beyond this life.

Of course many more hints of the continuance of life might be added in this same line. But all these evidences of immortality are insignificant compared to one other. The human heart longs

for a "Thus saith the Lord." Do we not have
it in "Jesus Christ, who hath abolished death,
and hath brought life and immortality to light
through the gospel"? Some one has called attention to the contrast between the thought of
immortality among the early Christians and their
pagan neighbors. The surrounding pagan world
rested under the black shadow of scepticism.
With the Christians the future world was almost
as certain as this one. Paul voices the faith of
the early church when he says, "For we know,
that if our earthly house of this tabernacle were
dissolved, we have a building of God, a house
not made with hands, eternal in the heavens."
Travellers tell us that in the Catacombs, where
are both Christian and pagan tombs, the Christian are distinguished by the greater faith of the
epitaph. If those early Christians had not seen
the risen Lord, or any one who had seen him,
they had testimony sufficiently at first hand to
make his resurrection a certainty. So that open
sepulchre was to them, and in a measure is to us,
a kind of window in that cloud-gate in which
every earthly pathway ends.

But Jesus gives other evidence of immortality

scarcely less satisfactory than his reappearance among his disheartened disciples. There is disappointment sometimes that the Master did not say more about the immortal life. It is true that he does not say much specifically about it. He does not even use the word "immortality," or the phrases "immortal life," or "future life." But is there not very gratifying teaching in this sience? He assumes the doctrine of immortality to be true. That is a very strong conviction of the truth of a doctrine that assumes it to be true. It suggests what a certainty immortality was to Jesus that he did not think it necessary to argue about it, or try to prove it. In that pathetic conversation with his shadowed disciples on the eve of the great tragedy, he said, " In my Father's house are many mansions: *if it were not so I would have told you.*"

The source of this certainty we do not know. It may be that he was so far up the mount of holiness, and so near to God, that he could hear the whispers of the divine. Certainly he could not have been mistaken, and thought he knew when he did not know. A certain writer says, " If one tells me ninety-nine truths, I will trust

him in the hundredth, especially if it is involved
in those before. When the clearest eye that ever
looked on the world and into the heavens, and
the keenest judgment that ever weighed human
life, and the purest heart that ever throbbed with
human sympathy, tells me, especially if he tells
it by assumption, that man is immortal, I repose
on his teaching in perfect trust."

After such a creditable witness to the existence of the immortal life, we may well pass on
to some consideration of the conditions of that
life. It may be thought that, if not presumptu-
ous, this cannot be a very satisfactory task ; that
the attempt to tell what kind of life awaits beyond the veil is like that of the author to describe an unvisited island of the sea. It is true,
as already intimated, that while the great Master
gives us good reason for believing in the immortal life, he nowhere attempts any portrayal of it.
The Scripture once thought to be descriptive of
the future life is now regarded by most competent
authority as illustrative of conditions in this life.
We sometimes wish that Jesus, if only for a
moment, had lifted the veil that hides so much
we long to see ; that he had left at least one

discourse on " Beyond the Gates , " that when he said, " In my Father's house are many mansions," he had given a detailed description of the heavenly house; that when he came back to his disciples he had told them all about the land he had just visited, and to which he would soon return. There is a spot on the highlands back of Lake Erie, where that magnificent stretch of landscape that borders the lake opens to the traveller journeying toward it all at once. The first time I came to that spot, I stood entranced before the wondrous scene, — grainfields, apple orchards, peach orchards, vineyards, beautiful homes, so suddenly revealed. So perhaps the landscapes of heaven wait to entrance us with the suddenness of the view.

And yet imagination is not without aid here. It is not true that the gospel tells us nothing of the character of the immortal life. While the great Teacher does not lift the veil from before our longing eyes, his attitude toward it is very suggestive of what is on the other side. It has been said that the fact that Jesus so infrequently refers especially to the immortal life, strongly evidences the existence of that life. Is it not

also suggestive as to the character of that life?
Certainly were the immortal world entirely different from this morally, under different laws,
with different rewards and penalties, Jesus would
have told us all about it. The fact that he
says so little about the immortal life, especially
the fact that he is so largely concerned with
making men happy here, shows that he did not
distinguish between this and the next life; that
in his mind the immortal, intellectually and morally at least, is essentially a continuance of this
present life. And why must not this be the
case? The intellectual and moral nature survives. Death is merely the removal of the spiritual tenant out of the material house into the
house not made with hands. The real person
is no more essentially affected by the change
than is a person by removal from one house into
another. The mind and heart, the will and conscience, remain the same. Therefore death is not
a gateway into a foreign country, where a divine
government unlike what we are acquainted with
here prevails. Man enters the immortal world
to find the same divine government that has always ruled him; barring material temptations, the
same moral relations as in this life.

The good and bad are not materially separated
in this world. They live together in the same
community. The noble and ignoble touch elbows
on the street, deal with each other, yea, sleep
under the same roof, and eat at the same table.
God does not reward the righteous here with an
outward paradise, nor punish the wicked with
exile into some awful place. The divine government here is administered within the soul. The
kingdom of God is within us. It cannot be different in the immortal life. Man enters the immortal world not to find some place of reward or
punishment prepared for him, but to experience
whatever of heaven or hell within himself his pre-
vious life has prepared him for. The gateway of
death must open into a blessed heaven for him
who has made the most of his life. But how can
he who has lived mostly for the material here,
when entirely separated from it, find other, at first,
than a most barren life? He whose disposition
has not permitted happiness in this world will
scarcely enter at once into unalloyed bliss in the
next. He who does not find the backward look
pleasant from the summit of this life, because of
the faults and follies that mar the scene, from the

heights of the immortal will scarcely find it more
so. Indeed, under that whiter light will it not
be less satisfactory than before?

But with the same divine government, the
same Saviour, the same will and conscience, there
must be the same opportunity of salvation in the
immortal world as here. The sinful soul can no
more lose its opportunity of repentance and reformation by entering the next world than by emi-
gration to France. Indeed, with its freedom from
earthly temptation, salvation must be easier in
that life. Can you conceive of a soul, however
sinful here, in the larger spiritual freedom and
light of the immortal life, with no more pleading
of the earthly appetite or impulse of evil passion,
remaining long out of the right way? Is not all
this very comforting, especially in view of the
many who have had but poor chance of growth
in grace here? A certain gentleman has said
that he never walks through the poorer quarters
of his city, past the crowded tenement houses,
and looks at the little ragged forms and starved,
pinched faces at the windows and doorways, without a great thankfulness for the thought that
these unfortunates are to have another and better
chance for their lives.

The thought that the immortal world is not divided into two localities, one of reward and another of penalty, suggests the question, What is it outwardly like? The statement now so often heard, that heaven and hell are conditions, not places, is likely to create the unsatisfactory and unreasonable idea that the immortal world is "without form and void." Emerson speaks of Swedenborg having taken an important step in religious history when he taught a future world with the accompaniments of all nature, where should be continued "the like employments in the like circumstances as those we know;" and quotes Milton as saying, "What if earth be but the shadow of heaven and things therein, each to the other like more than on earth is thought." Certainly it is not a very satisfactory conception of the future world that does not locate it, nor give it any form or feature; that pictures departed spirits as shadows drifting on a sea of space. We have been made to enjoy this material world. We delight in the forms of nature, — the hills, the lakes, the streams, the trees, the flowers. Would our nature permit satisfaction with a world where there is nothing like these?

Some writer has said, "Three things there must be in heaven, — children and music and flowers."

This suggests the question, Why may not liberated spirits still remain amid these material scenes they have loved? Why should we think of the immortal world as in some distant realm of space? I like the old illustration of the immortal life drawn from the transformation that results in a butterfly. The butterfly sheds his husk, not to find himself in another world, but still in the old world, with increased capacity to use and enjoy it; the power to rise into the sunshine, and find the flowers. Why may not death be, not transportation, but transformation in a sense, — birth out of the material, yet into the same old world, with new visions and uses of it? The poet says : —

> " So sometimes comes to soul and sense
>   The feeling which is evidence
>   That very near about us lies
>   The realm of spiritual mysteries.
>   The sphere of the supernal powers
>   Impinges on this world of ours."

The thought that the spirit world may be right here gives rise to an old and perplexing question. Must not its happiness often be spoiled by the miseries of earth? How can the mother, amid whatever sources of delight, find it heaven, knowing that the little ones whose heartstrings were so interwoven with hers that in all their sufferings she herself felt a pang, are being neglected and abused? It has been well asked whether she would be any happier ignorant of their fate. May it not be said that earthly suffering cannot appear to immortal as mortal eyes? The mother in heaven knows not only that while the weeping of her child may endure for a night, joy cometh in the morning, but perhaps sees how his light affliction, which is but for a moment, works for him a " far more exceeding and eternal weight of glory."

But let us consider briefly some other features of the immortal life. It is a common conception of heaven, often expressed in sermon and song, that it is "a land of rest." " There the wicked cease from troubling, and there the weary be at rest." Says a beautiful sacred song, " Up above the stars there is rest." Of course the immortal world cannot impose the burdens of toil that the earthly pilgrim often longs to lay down. A realm without material necessities must be without many of the labors of this life, and no work in such a world can be the severe taskmaster it often is here. There the body does not wear out from the friction of hard work; the back does not ache under burdens too heavy for it; the fingers do not stiffen with the severity of their tasks. "What shall we eat, and what shall we drink, and wherewithal shall we be clothed?" is no longer a harassing anxiety. Of many a one who enters the immortal life, it must be blessedly true that "he rests from his labors."

And yet would that life be satisfactory were there no kind of labor there? Human nature was made for activity. Inactivity soon ceases to be rest. Many persons are miserable in this world from having nothing to do. How wearisome would the immortal life become with no other pursuit than singing God's praise! Think of the mind which has been especially active here, that has found its very life in excursions through these wondrous realms of thought, being happy in a world where there is nothing to think about! Is it heaven to Agassiz if he can no longer pursue his favorite sciences? Is it not darkness to Herschel if he is shut out from the light of the stars? Is Longfellow happy if there is no inspiration to song?

Is there any reason why there should not be as good an opportunity in the immortal life of intellectual and moral activity as here? The necessity for men to instruct and make better themselves and others must furnish ample exercise for all. It may be that the opportunities of knowledge will be so much greater that all will become delighted students there. I recall a discourse in which the preacher referred to the new opportunities that the immortal life will give to science. He thought that there may not be any impediment to transit in that life. And why should not the celestial inhabitant have all the freedom of the skies? Why should he not visit the outermost world of space, and test for himself Mr. Proctor's wondrous picture of far-away worlds, clothed in ever-changing loveliness under colored suns? Perhaps with the material veil removed, the immortal spirit may see this marvellous mechanism of force about us, the, to us, unseen loom that weaves the flowers.

But there is a more important consideration with respect to the immortal life. It concerns its social relations. The probability of recognizing friends in the immortal life has been a much-discussed theme. Certainly it will be practically annihilation if we do not retain conscious identity, and as little desirable if we do not know each other. The greatest good of this world results from its friendships and kinships. Of what value would this world be to you if all the cords were cut that bind you to others? Chapin said, "The most lonely of beings is a man cut off from all social relations and domestic ties. The rock that stands out in the ocean alone with the sky and the surf is only an image of human desolation. . . . There is nothing so solitary as a solitary man." Whatever the attractions of the immortal life, though its sky be fairer than any overarching the earth, though its landscapes be more charming than any that have ever inspired the painter's brush, it must be desolation if friend does not meet with friend. No thought of that life so quickens the pulses as that those to whom we so reluctantly said good-night are waiting' to bid us a glad good-morning, when we shall awaken from the sleep of death into that eternal day.

But how can disembodied spirits know each other? Here we recognize each other very largely, though not wholly, by form and feature. How can we know each other when these bodies have been laid aside to crumble to their parent dust? "How are the dead raised up, and with what body do they come?" Paul says, "There is a natural body and there is a spiritual body." Stopford Brooke says, "If we believe in God at all, that a new form should knit itself to a mind and spirit which have become personal through the memories and worth of a human life, is no more incredible than that they should have been originally knit together." Many years ago, in his famous Analogy, Bishop Butler taught what has since been more specifically illustrated by the scientific believer, — that there is not only a spiritual body, but with the same form as the natural body. It has been said, in opposition to materialism, that instead of the body giving birth to the spirit, the spirit originates the body. Why may not the 'material body be a garment which the soul has woven for itself? If the body be a mantle draped about the spiritual form, then when it is torn away by the hand of death, the form will remain.

What a comforting thought it is that we shall see
again the same familiar form, greet again the same
beloved face that faded into the darkness, in
whose very expression there was such comfort,
inspiration, and joy!

What a wonderful thought this is of the immortal life! Many grand conceptions have resulted
from the human mind. But grander than any
machinery it has invented, grander than any of
its thoughts of the marvels of space, is this
thought of immortal life. What a thought it is
that you and I will never cease to be; that the
scenes we have known and the friends we have
enjoyed we shall always know and enjoy; that
life is an endless highway; death, as some one has
called it, "a covered bridge." We pass through
to overtake those who have gone on in advance of
us, and in their blessed companionship, dearer and
sweeter than was possible here, because there are
no longer any differences of opinion to alienate, any
earthly struggles and trials to irritate, — in their
blessed companionship to go on and up forever,
with constantly new visions and new joys. Who
can think of it without increased respect for himself, without feeling that a being of such noble lin-

eage and destiny is too good to live an unworthy life? Remembering that "the pure in heart see God," that "spiritual things are spiritually discerned," we should so live that the immortal life will be a constant reality to us.

A PERFECTED CHARACTER: THE GOAL OF LIFE.

FRED AUGUSTINE DILLINGHAM.

A PERFECTED CHARACTER: THE GOAL OF LIFE.

1. *Life.*

HUMAN life is a problem, in its present estate, in its mediate and ultimate destiny; and the problem grows as our consciousness of its elements increases. In its lowest conception it involves struggle, and pronounces its interrogatory, " How shall life be sustained ? " As the conception broadens, struggles increase, and questions multiply in number and interest. In its lowest forms the attainment of temporary physical comfort is about the only thought and effort. When man recognizes the relationships and interdependencies of physical functions, the question becomes, how to harmonize, how to lubricate, the various bearings, that the machine may run without friction.

The dawning consciousness of intellectual faculties and need still further complicates the problem; and in the gratification and growth of these powers, in the provision for these needs, life rises to a higher dignity, realizes a larger usefulness, and returns a sweeter blessing.

So with the recognition of the powers and claims of our social, moral, æsthetic, and spiritual being. Each forward step carries us farther into the problem; each upward step increases labor, adds responsibility, presents new and more difficult problems. At the same time our horizon of life is broadening, fresh delights open along the way, new realms of knowledge come within our range; and the exhilarating, inspiring advance upon the heights grants the sweetest satisfactions, and promotes the largest health and growth. Human life is not only a problem; it is an individual, personal problem. The spirit and accomplishment of the life depend upon a personal comprehension of its powers and possibilities. A large vision of life's power is not always the assurance of large accomplishment; but no large accomplishment can come without the large vision. *It is the prime essential.* The first thing for the individual to do in preparing for life is to take an honest view of the situation, face his conditions, and take an inventory of his personal estate. By an honest view we mean accepting the universal testimony of the senses, universal intuitions, and the brightest light of discovery and revelation. What is man? Physically he is an animal; i.e., with organs, adjustments, needs, desires, which, properly supplied, conduce to physical health, growth, reproduction, and comfort. But more than this, the physical man is adjusted to minister to the higher faculties of mind and soul, and through these in return to receive a ministration which exalts merely animal *comfort* to human *happiness*.

Man is soul; he is an emanation from God; he is God's child; he has God-given faculty and capacity; he is God-like in the quality of intellect, affection, and will, in moral and spiritual instincts and powers; he has capacity and desire for the *exercise* of all these faculties.

How is man conditioned? He is placed in a physical realm that is friendly, that readily furnishes all needed supply for physical life and growth, — an ample sphere filled with plenteous stores of material to captivate the eye, delight the æsthetic sense, stimulate and enlarge the intellect, and enlist the affections, — opportunities, necessarily exercising the will, realms for testing the social and moral powers. And to-day not only the leadings of a universal spiritual intuition, but the revelations to the spirit, the experiences of the race, and the discoveries of nature's harmonies, assure man of his relationship to and dependence upon God, — of the immortality of the soul, and of his relations and duties to man.

Life means not only a recognition, but activity, of the faculties. Activity is natural, and is induced by the necessary conditions of contact with earth. The infant lungs are congested, and leap into action by contact with air. The eyes are called into action by light, and the ears by sound. The demands of the new relation create hunger, under conditions which provide supply. The intellect dawns by contact with that upon which it feeds. Love feels its impulse; the will, moral and spiritual faculties, assert themselves under the divine provision of nature. Natural activity involves neither pain nor loss, but suspended activity involves both. It is natural and easy to breathe, unnatural and harmful to cease. It is natural and easy to think, sometimes impossible to stop. Natural and easy to will and love, unnatural and harmful to impede the action of either. It is natural to have and exercise moral sense and spiritual aspiration, unnatural and withering to suppress them.

Life means the healthy, natural exercise of powers. Growth, whether physical, intellectual, moral, or spiritual, is dependent upon health. The study of men discovers how inadequate has been the comprehension of the marvellous powers of life. Men have failed to see life in its fulness of power, in its wealth of endowment, in its varied functions, in its myriad adaptations.

The most noticeable thing in a survey of human life is its lack of symmetry. The average human life is so different from its design and possibility, even in its contour. The divinely beautiful tree has been deprived of nourishment or sun; its budding powers have been sadly and ruthlessly closed; the tap-root running into the soil of the Infinite has been partially, and often practically, sealed up. A few wild, unsightly, and barren branches too often confront us, in place of the divinely beautiful, natural, and symmetrical tree filled with, and contributing to, life.

No one can take a calm, thoughtful view of

life without being filled with wonder and astonishment at its marvellous mechanical design; its
eloquent scope; its range of faculty, extending
from the needed ministry of the physical to the
no less needed ministry of the spiritual; its adjustments for time and for eternity; its commu-
nions with Nature and with Nature's God. We
are possessed with wonder when we view the
complex and mammoth machines of human skill.
We view with growing astonishment the suns
and systems of God's physical universe. We fall
down in awe before the vision of God's gift of
life to man, which in design, in skill, in adjustment, in possibility, is God's masterpiece.

II. *The Goal.*

Life is not an accident, but a design. The possession of a "governor" by a machine is a presumption that it has a purpose, and that it has a
sphere of action; so with the condenser, there is
something to be condensed, some need of conden-
sation for the success of the work. The existence
of this — God's masterpiece — is a presumption of
purpose, of legitimacy. That God is all-powerful
creates a profound respect and expectation con-

cerning his work. The work itself commands our
wonder. That God is all-wise forces the conviction that this work is purposeful and resultful;
that he is all goodness assures us of its beneficent
design in relation to himself, itself, and the world;
that he is all-loving confirms our hope that the
results will be felicitously consummated. The
existence of life is not only the pledge of a divine
purpose or goal, but the wealth of human faculty
sheds light upon the wide extent of realms that
are tributary to this result. The existence of
each faculty is God's guaranty that it has a part
to act in the drama of the soul's existence. The
possession of physical being is the assurance of
its divine relation to the goal. The possession of
intellect is God's command to us to use it in the
service of life. The possession of will and affection command their exercise. The leadings of
instincts mark the way. The thirsts of the spirit
conduct to the fountain of soul-supply, and bid us
partake. Again the power of our endowment, the
observed accomplishments of life, are a prophetic
gleam of the magnitude of God's purpose. The
glow of conscious physical power and health;
the reaches and triumphs of intellect, in whose

crown rest the wonders of the microscopic atom and the glories of the telescopic sphere; the inspiration of love, under power of which hearts and homes have given birth to society and nation, in whose embrace the families and kindred of the earth find a place, and whose altars burn with the spirit of helpfulness for a universe of souls; the power of will in shaping the destinies of men and nations; the artistic skill that has wrought such wonders; the æsthetic sense that has so persistently and helpfully ministered to the every stage and condition of life; the moral sense that has directed and held sway in the vicissitudes of individual, social, and national struggles; the spiritual impulse and uplift that has left no man without a present help, no nation without a God, and has been as the beacon of hope to the storm-tossed, a haven of rest to the weary, — these are the earnest of a sublime, divine purpose.

While a careful survey of life gives no uncertain sound regarding the existence of a *divine* purpose, it gives sadly eloquent testimony that many men have failed to apprehend that fact, many more have failed to be inspired by it, and most have failed to comprehend its nature, its breadth, or its complete harmony. Many have never been awakened from the earth-long sleep of physical existence; or, if aroused, have gained but an indistinct vision of higher glories, and have lapsed into slumber. Others have stood temporarily upon the heights where the delights of the intellect, the pulsings of the will, the throb of love, the sense of moral responsibility, or the ecstasy of spiritual reality have swept over and through them, only to close these divine avenues through lack of purpose. Still others, having tasted the sweets of either the physical, intellectual, affectional, moral, or spiritual realm, have closed their eyes to all others; and thus recklessly have destroyed, not only the symmetry of growth, but have withheld from life the rich fruitage of a developed whole, and have failed to realize the richest possibilities of the *chosen* field.

The successes of life are only attained by purpose. Chance winds may blow an occasional blossom across our path, but they never cultivate flowers. Whatever has been achieved in any of the wide domains of life has been born of an aim; some end in view has lured and cheered and strengthened the toiler on his way. The aimless man is not only unproductive, he is a burden to himself and society, he is one of the serious problems in modern civilization; he has to be supported, if not with the necessities of existence, surely by the many provisions of a wise society; he is not a *power*, but a *pensioner* in society, in business, and in everything that draws strength from the higher realm of life. Looking at the activities and the accomplishments of life — all the results of purpose — we cannot fail to be impressed with the conviction that there has been strong purpose acting as the lever of the world's progress, and also that the purposes of men have a wonderful variety and intensity. The accomplishments of good that dot the pages of human history and mark its glory are eloquent testimonies and hopeful prophecies, and its increasing army of devotees to the good, the beautiful, and the true, and its steady advance in the realms of knowledge and life, mark the still nearer and nearing approach of the purposes of men to the purpose of God; while the accomplishments of evil, seen as such by the good, and largely acknowledged as such by the workers of evil, remain as problems, although carrying in their bosoms the weapons of their own destruction in the confession of their selfish purpose and greed.

The dominance of legitimate purposes in the activities of life marks our hopeful advance. Still, the goals of life as viewed and pursued by men in the direction of progress are sadly inadequate, oftentimes they cross purposes from a lack of harmonious action. No adequate purpose of life can be formed by confining our vision to one faculty or sphere of life. Our faculties are interdependent. Our *highest* motive comes of a recognition of all faculties, and a desire to so adjust them, one to the other, each to all, that the harmony may be secured. The history of life testifies to the preponderance of partial and individual motives in the struggles of life. Partial views, partial activities, have withered the crop, or produced fruit inferior in quality and quantity for the world's sustenance. Results have been only partially satisfying. It is not possible for a partial success to satisfy man; it is not possible for the man whose only success is the attainment of physical health and comfort to feel satisfied. The ascent of intellectual heights while other realms are untried or unknown is inadequate to

human need. Wealth, fame, position, all have
been sought, and all, notwithstanding their worth,
when weighed in the balance with man's needs,
are found wanting. There are goodly pearls in
any of the many fields of life ; no one of which,
however, is worthy to rest "solitaire" in the
crown of life ; but all are worthy a place in the
setting of the pearl of great price, from whose
surpassing lustre each gains an added value and
increased beauty.

Not only is there a great diversity of aims in
human life, but the various stages of the same life
may be, and often are, marked by radical changes
in purpose. The goal the child sets before himself, and which for the time holds him in en-
thusiastic adherence for its attainment, gives place
to a new purpose under his broadening vision and
ripening experience, which in turn is supplanted
by another. What is true in childhood is true,
in lesser extent, in youth, still true in the least
degree in age. What more natural ; what more
necessary? Youthful vision, limited observation,
brief experience, in the study of life, give short
range to the goal, the pleasurable is seen as desirable, and it is seen as near ; but, with the

awakening of the larger powers, the field broadens, the ambitions take a loftier flight, experience deepens our purpose, and the goal is still at a remoter distance, calling for greater and longer continued devotion in a pathway beset with difficulties. Thus the cultivation of our powers, the feeding of our faculties, conduce to a breadth of purpose which, while it dethrones the small usurpers of life's little kingdoms, elevates them to the peerage in the larger government of the larger kingdom of life.

III. *Character.*

Among the aims that have actuated human life, character holds conspicuous place. A character is a mark, and as applied to life is the way or groove, cut out by one's self, in which to move. Character, whether good or bad, is a commanding force. But as evil forces are temporary by nature and necessity, having the whole power of internal, external, and eternal means to subdue them, we shall consider only character as directed to a permanent good. Character is not nature, it is not primitive natural impulse, it is not a gift from God; it is a human product; it cannot be purchased from another, or put on as a garment; it cannot be transferred; it is something attained; it is a creation, a growth; it is not a transient impulse, but a stable habit. Nature is God's gift to us; character is our gift to God. Nature furnishes the material; character is the human product. Character is the verdict we pronounce upon the problem of life; it represents our solution. Character represents, not possession of the things of the world, but the possession of one's self. It is not expressed in the things acquired, but in the principle or method of acquisition. The stronghold of character is that it recognizes the supremacy of right, and that its kingdom is within us. Nature questions how to obtain food for its impulses; character studies how these shall be fed to insure health and growth. Character interrogates life's impulses, and asks, not what does appetite seek, but what will satisfy and bless. Character asks of intellect, as it stands on the border land of rich territory, not how much can be gathered of whatsoever kind, but what can be gleaned to contribute to intellectual power and life's largest good. Character discriminates, it sifts, it adjudicates, it rules, on the conviction of permanent good.

The ideal of highest good has varied in the ages
and stages of human progress. Character has
been manifested and expressed in many ways, but
it always has the mark of a definite purpose and
method to serve what is believed to be good.

Scientists tell us that magnetism is not a foreign something that is imparted to a bar of iron,
whereby it is made magnetic, but that magnetism
is a native quality of iron, or a particular arrangement of its atoms. Science says that magnetization
simply rearranges the atoms, and that a bar of iron
is magnetic in character when the atoms are so
arranged that the *inherent magnetic quality leads.*
Human character is formed, not by importing a
foreign substance, but by a definite arrangement
of faculties. Characters productive of evil come
by elevating to the throne of power and the position of leadership an infirm, perverted, or naturally
tributary impulse. Characters productive of good
come from such an arrangement of our faculties
and powers in life that the higher permanent faculties shall lead. Men are characterized in fact
and in reputation generally by their leading motive. Some men are intellectually polarized; they
feel that the intellectual *realm* is superior, that

intellectual *needs* are superior, and that intellectual *attainments* are supreme. Others have a volitional or affectional polarization, others have an æsthetic polarity, still others moral or spiritual. And all these characteristics are seen with their numerous radiations as they reach out into the varied and rich fields of human thought and activity. Character has various qualities, dependent upon whether inspired by the ideas of happiness, utility, or absolute right. Characters have assurance in varying degrees, dependent upon the recognized source of power, whether as in the individual or in the race or in the Supreme Spirit. Characters have scope and power dependent upon the conviction of life as temporal or eternal.

At this stage of advancement in human life, it cannot be seriously doubted that the highest character is marked by the Christian purpose to serve right, reposing in its assurance of birth from and government by the infinite God, and reading its destiny in immortality. The influences that have operated all through human history to crystallize purpose into character have been numerous and mighty; the persistent and unrelenting impulse of the soul, which has never allowed man to

rest satisfied save in right; the harmonies of physical, intellectual, moral, and spiritual life that
have gradually lifted men into a vision and appreciation of rightness and wholeness; the undying
influence of manifested good and truth and beauty
as it has shone upon us from the hilltops of life,
in saint, sage, psalmist, and prophet — not in any
one, but in *all* ages of the world — and especially
in the life of Jesus Christ. Truly the angel of the
Lord has not only been encamped round about
man, but has kept vigil at his inner tent, — the
Holy of Holies. As a contribution to, and as a
direct and all-powerful influence in, crystallizing
human character, the life and teaching of Jesus
Christ stand as unique. In the teachings of Jesus
the world gets its first grand and inspiring knowledge of the Universal Father. This vision of divine origin, divine and imperishable love, divine
and unending guardianship, and of divine purpose,
at once laid the necessary and permanent foundation of enduring purpose in man. Man then saw
himself divine, divined, and capable of divining.
In the gospel the world first saw the reality of universal brotherhood and what it involved. Then
the world held the sufficient evidence, legitimizing

the existence and purpose of all power, and commanding a husbandry of all resources. In the life of Jesus, truly the Word (" gospel ") made flesh, the living, practising, illustrating personality, the world first saw the picture of life as God designed it, as man should view it and live it. Once seen, it has been recognized by the world as the sublime ideal and manifestation of life. Its prophecies in dull outline had long blessed the world and fed its hope. Its copies, drawn in all succeeding time, with varying degrees of perfection, testify to its matchless beauty, its supreme inspiration, and its *mastery still.* It is the crowning manifestation of character, recognized as such the world over. It is the crowning inspiration to human thought and effort, as advancing Christian civilization testifies. Christian character, the character that comprehends the gospel principle and exemplifies gospel virtues, is the type before which the world bends in grateful homage, and in which reposes its fondest hope.

IV. *A Perfected Character.*

We are apt to think of anything as perfected when completed, when it has reached its possibility, when it is *full*, incapable of further addition or improvement. Thus viewed, the question arises, " Can a character be perfect? " Can there be attained such a completeness that nothing further is desirable or possible? Can a character attain its growth at any time or period so that beyond it there is no change? This is not a frivolous speculation, but it has distinct and forceful bearing on the deep questions of time and eternity. If life means growth, if time means opportunity for growth, and full growth is attained by any soul, of what service is the balance of eternity to that soul? It would seem to thus have outstripped the infinite design, or outdone the divine expectation. Absolute perfection is an ideal, and not to humanity an accomplished or accomplishable thing, if thus popularly viewed. Certain it is that no known life on the earth has reached such a stage of completeness. We have had great specialists in the various fields of human accomplishment; but we have never seen an all-round, all-rounded, fully developed life, i.e., one exhausting human possibility. We have had great warriors, weak in morals. We have had wise philosophers, dwarfed in spirit. We have

had specialists in the knowledge of earth, ignorant
of the stars; wise scientists who could control
many of earth's forces, still ignorant of self-con-
trol. And at the best, no warrior, philosopher,
geographer, or scientist has the world seen, who
held *undisputed the title of ruler.* — no one who
had in any way exhausted the possibilities of his
faculties or the field of research. We have had
great and wise instructors in morals and religion;
still, how incomplete has seemed the world's systems in both realms. The systems have largely
been proven incomplete and faulty. Look at the
teachers themselves, even the *founders* of moral
and religious systems, and see, under growing
light of the world, how imperfect most appear,
how weak in comprehension and in government.
In its comprehension and character Christianity
rises mountain high above the summits of ordinary hills. No! — earth has not produced absolute completion in the development of human life.
If by perfection we mean reaching that point
beyond which no more is possible, perfection becomes *impossible* except as an idea, by the law
of life, the opportunity of life, and the duration
of life, which point to endless progression.

We might fancy that a science, the possession of whose secrets made one a pre-eminent teacher on earth, might be exhausted under a few æons of eternity; still, when we think that to know any one thing thoroughly, one must know all things, the day of perfect knowledge is pushed into the dim eternity. We might think that one who had learned in time or in the young days of eternity to know of the existence of the infinite God, and to apprehend his love for his children, might become perfected in spiritual motive and power and service in the opening *cycles* of eternity. But when we reflect what it means to know God as he knows us, to grow to a full possession of infinite compassion, to be perfect in everything, the day of absolute perfection recedes. If history can be trusted, perfection — absolute, entire fulness in everything — has never appeared on earth. When Enoch walked with God, when Abraham was commanded to be perfect, the eternity-long ideal was not brought before them, but something they were to, and could, accomplish while in the flesh, in the process of development, in a still imperfect condition. Job i. 1 says the man of Uz was " perfect and upright," but a study of the character will impress the fact that *absolute* fulness of knowledge and being was not and could not be postulated of him. The injunction of Jesus to his disciples, " Be ye therefore perfect, even as your Father which is in heaven is perfect," was certainly not to encourage the disciples in the hope or expectancy of becoming equal with God. His word to the rich young man, who had kept all the commandments from his youth up, " If thou wilt be perfect, go sell that thou hast, and give to the poor." cannot possibly be construed as identifying added thoughtfulness and ministry to the poor with absolute character-perfection, meaning completion or fulness. Even the character which we all so much delight to ascribe to Jesus himself as the perfect man, the perfect teacher, the perfect Saviour, must be taken with a restricted meaning, certainly not in its absolute fulness. Jesus said, " I can of mine own self do nothing; " that is certainly not a claim of absolute perfection, meaning fulness of power. He said there were things he did not know; that certainly limits absolute fulness of knowledge. Not to detract, heaven forbid! one jot or one tittle from the supreme glory of Jesus Christ as man or teacher or Saviour, not to deny or doubt any claim he made for himself, not to detract from the popular apprehension of his exalted sphere, but in absolute fidelity to what we believe he taught and was. Perfection thus seen is an ideal, ultimate product, a goal towards which we look for inspiration, towards which we work, but never attain.

The terms "perfect," "perfection," and "perfected," are most commonly used, not in this sense of absolute completeness, but in an accommodated sense, referring to quality rather than quantity, or again referring to stages of development rather than full development, also as referring to a promise of good rather than accomplished good. A tone may be perfect in quality without reference to volume or range, which may be soft or harsh, high or low. The rich young man was told how to increase the quality of his life in the earth. He was devout, obedient to God and man, virtuous; he needed the quality of mercy, not to complete his character and accomplishment, or bring it to that point beyond which there was no growth, but to give it Christian quality, to fit it to *be* and to *do* better things.

We speak of perfection in the bud, the blossom, and even in the unripe fruit, in this qualitative way, and with reference to its promise of further development. We speak of infancy, childhood, youth, manhood, and age in terms of perfection, referring to qualities that in the highest degree characterize the *stages* of development. How much is embraced in the fact of Jesus' perfection we cannot now know; we certainly believe that not only the *quality* of his life was the most perfect, i.e., most like God's, that the world has ever seen or shall see, but that in a peculiar way there was a larger, more perfect *range* of conscious power, a more perfect *harmonious blending* of *faculties*, a more perfect *subjection* of the lesser, a more perfect exaltation of the greater powers, than the world has seen.

There was perfect oneness with God in the *quality* of life, " the brightness of God's glory and the express image [χαρακτήρ] of his person." Jesus had, and represented to the world, in a pre-eminent and appointed way the *quality* of a divinely balanced life, actually as in God, potentially as in man.

So perfect was this life, so true a representation,

that it is, and is to be, the goal of earthly inspiration, — the undimmed pattern to point our search,
and stimulate our activity.

The "polarity" of Jesus' life was spiritual, and
thus discloses the *perfect, divine order* and *proces-
sion* by which souls advance in harmonious and
endless progress. Thus held, the idea of a perfected character takes its place as a *legitimate* goal
of life. ·It is harmonious with the revealed
powers and purposes of God, that find expression,
not only in his word, but in his work, in the almost
infinite capacity of human faculty, in the scope of
human power, in the duration of soul-life, and in
the *quality* of its fruits.

It is harmonious with the innate and undying
desire of man to attain the best.

No man is permanently satisfied with imperfection in anything which he may undertake.

Earnest life is marked by inspection, retrospec-
tion, prospection, and a purpose to improve.

A vision of that which is true and beautiful
and good stimulates effort for its attainment ; and
each attempt, when found to be imperfect, serves
as a stepping-stone and spur for greater advance.

A soul is never satisfied when it has less than

the recognition and activity of *all* its powers, when it has anything less than the highest revealed ideal of divine and human service, anything less than spiritual quality and leadership, anything less than advancement in a symmetrical, spiritual development. It is harmonious with the idea of its possibility; since what God has so clearly marked out as his purpose in human life, and what universal man, as constituted and born of God, desires, must be *possible*.

It is harmonious with *facts* as testified to in human experience, and in the multitude of lives, which, patterned after the Saviour, have helped to lift, ennoble, and fructify the sources and forces of human power, whereof the knowledge, virtue, and joy of Christian civilizations eloquently testify.